Jane's

Teachers' Safety Guide

Rita Duda
Sonayia Shepherd
Mike Dorn
Marleen Wong
Greg Thomas

Published by Jane's Information Group
Sentinel House
163 Brighton Road, Coulsdon
Surrey CR5 2YH, UK
Tel: +44 (0) 20 8700 3700
Fax: +44 (0) 20 8763 1006
e-mail: info@janes.com

Printed in the United States

Registered with the Library of Congress

Cataloging-in-Publication Data available upon request

ISBN 07106 26606

Editorial and Project Management
Content Developer: *Rob Fanney*

Editorial
Content Developer: *Seth Drewry*
Content Developer: *Mary Dinh*
Consultancy Manager: *Rennie Campbell*
Consultancy Manager: *Jim Tinsley*

Graphic Design
Senior Design Manager: *Steve Allen*
Photo editor: *Julie Medlock*
Graphic Designer: *Steve Allen*
Graphic Designer: *Bethany Hackmann*

Production
Group Content Director: *Anita Slade*
Global Production Services Manager: *Jane Lawrence*
Production Services: *Natalie Wilson*
Page Layout: *Land & Unwin*
Photos: Senior Design Manager: *Steve Allen*

Administration
Content Development Manager: *Ian Synge*
Business Development Director: *Michael Dell*
Chief Executive Officer: *Alfred Rolington*

Publisher's Note

Jane's would like to thank the authors of *Jane's Teachers' Safety Guide.*

Rita Duda – Rita Duda is the lead editor and writer of this guide. She worked tirelessly to develop this guide so it will be useful for teachers. Rita is a Visiting Adjunct Professor of Literacy at the College of Education and Human Services at Cleveland State University. She also served on the review panel for the other products in the *Jane's School Safety Suite*. A retired Reading and Literacy teacher for the Cleveland Municipal School district, Cleveland, Ohio, she has over 25 years of experience in the classroom dealing with community spillover: gangs, crime, illegal narcotics and family disintegration. She also served as a full-time Peer Advisor consultant for new teachers to the Cleveland Municipal School district.

Sonayia Shepherd – Sonayia "Sony" Shepherd was an indispensable asset to the editorial team. Sony, who provided support in developing the mitigation and response sections, is a state government expert in bio-terrorism preparedness and training initiatives. She has broad-based experience in anti-terrorism, crisis recovery, school safety and victim's advocacy. She has authored or contributed to school safety guides, video training and a monthly column, "Sony Says" in *Campus Safety Journal*. She is certified in Adventure Therapy, Play Therapy, Juvenile and Adult Case Management, Managing Aggressive Behaviors, Crisis Intervention and Crisis Counseling.

Mike Dorn – Mike Dorn provided considerable contributions to the entire volume throughout the process. Michael Dorn is one of the nation's best known, most respected and highly credentialed school safety experts. A popular and powerful keynote speaker, Mr. Dorn has served in campus law enforcement and emergency management for 24 years with 10 years as a school system police chief, and as the lead expert for the nation's largest state government school safety center. In 2003, he accepted a key position in the Office of Homeland Security's antiterrorism division, Gerogia Emergency Management Agency (GEMA). He has authored and co-authored 18 books on school safety and his training videos are in use in 20 countries. He is a graduate of the FBI National Academy and received extensive antiterrorism training in Israel.

Marleen Wong – Marleen Wong, also lead editor, authored the chapter on recovery. Marleen is the Director of the School Crisis and Intervention Unit at UCLA and at Duke University. Identified by the Wall Street Journal as one of the "architects" of school safety programs, Ms. Wong has developed school crisis intervention teams and general mental health programs for school districts and law enforcement personnel in the United States, Canada and Asia. As a consultant to the US Department of Education, she has organized mental health recovery programs after many of the tragic school shootings and the terrorist attacks in Oklahoma City, New York and Washington, DC. Ms. Wong also serves on the National Academy of Sciences,

Institutes of Medicine Board on Neuroscience and Behavioral Health.

Gregory Thomas – Working as lead editor and leveraging his impressive knowledge and background, Gregory Thomas provided invaluable expertise and support throughout the process. One of the nation's top school safety experts, Gregory is currently the Director of the Program for School Preparedness and Planning in the National Center for Disaster Preparedness at Columbia University's Mailman School of Public Health. Mr. Thomas has over nineteen years experience in the public safety field and has served in such prestigious roles as: Executive Director of the Office of School Safety and Planning for the New York Department of Education, School Crisis and Intervention Unit of the National Center for Child Traumatic Stress Advisory Board member and as a member of US Department of State and Education select committees on school safety.

In addition to the authors, the following bestowed their considerable expertise and experience to the development and final review of the handbook:

Andrew A. Altizer – Andrew is an antiterrorism planner for a state homeland security agency. He has a BS in Criminal Justice from Truman State University and a MA in Educational Administration from the University of Missouri. He is also a public affairs officer with the National Guard.

Russell Bentley – A graduate of the FBI National Academy, Russell has been Chief of Campus Police for Bibb County Public Schools in Macon, Georgia for three years and has 18 years worth of Law Enforcement experience. Russell heads a group of law enforcement professionals nationally recognized as leaders in campus safety by the US Department of Education, U.S. Department of Justice Office of Justice Programs (OJJDP) and a number of other state and federal training agencies. Russell is a law enforcement instructor for the Criminal Justice Department of Central Georgia Technical College in Macon, Georgia.

Kelly Buddenhagen, NREMT-P – Kelly is the program coordinator for an Emergency Medical Services for Children. She has been in EMS for over ten years with a background in education and management. Before joining Georgia's Public Health team, she worked as a paramedic instructor as well as on an ambulance. A strong advocate for children, she spends her "spare" time teaching CPR and first aid to all ages and participates regularly as a car seat safety technician and pediatric education in her local community. Her education includes an Associates Degree in Emergency Medical Services and coursework in Emergency Management, Disaster Preparedness, Critical Incident training, Rescue, School Preparedness and Special Needs. An instructor in most of the Emergency Medical Courses, she is also responsible for bio-terrorism preparedness for pediatrics in a state government.

J. Kevin Cameron – J. Kevin Cameron, Director of the Canadian Center for Threat Assessment and Trauma Response, led the crisis response effort following Canada's first high profile school shooting in April, 1999 and, in concert with the RCMP Behavioral Sciences Unit, developed Canada's first multidisciplinary threat assessment training program.

Greg Champlin – Greg Champlin is the Natural Hazards Specialist with the New Hampshire Bureau of Emergency Management, primarily responsible for the agency's earthquake and hurricane programs. He also serves as interim public information officer and has done extensive work in news media relations, public outreach and disaster public information during emergencies. Greg has developed and has been conducting two-day Comprehensive Emergency Management Planning for Schools (CEMPS) workshops for school, community and emergency response personnel throughout New Hampshire for over a decade. He has also assisted other states in the implementation of CEMPS outreach activities. Greg is an adjunct faculty member at FEMA's Emergency Management Institute in Emittsburg, MD, the University of New Hampshire and Plymouth State University specializing in multi-hazard emergency planning for schools. He served with the US Coast Guard for five years, specializing in hazardous materials security and port inspection for two years. He has also been a volunteer firefighter and has managed and owned several businesses.

Julie Collins – Julie currently works as a Florida Department of Education School Safety Coordinator. Formerly, she held a position at the Florida Emergency Management Agency.

Adrian Dwyer – Lead editor and writer of *Jane's Chem-Bio Handbook International*, Adrian Dwyer has over 15 years of experience dealing with CBRN response issues, firstly as an Army bomb disposal officer and high-risk search adviser and secondly as the counter-terrorism advisor to the British Transport Police. Adrian is a member of the Risk and Security Management Forum and the Institute of Explosives Engineers. He holds an MSc in risk, crisis and disaster management and contributed to the 1999 *Jane's Chemical – Biological Defense Guidebook*.

Will Evans – Will is currently the Director of Safety Education for the Markell Insurance company. Will has extensive experience in the risk management and safety training fields.

Louie Fernandez – Louie Fernandez is a Senior Bureau Chief for Public Affairs with Miami-Dade County's Fire Rescue (MDFR) and Office of Emergency Management (OEM) and lead editor of *Jane's Crisis Communications Handbook*.

Dr. Ted Feinburg – Dr. Feinburg is currently serving as the Assistant Director of the National Association of School Nurses.

Bob Howard is Co-Chairman of the CDC's AITT First Annual Automated Identification and Tracking Technology Conference. For twelve years, Bob served as Director of Strategic Communications at the National Center for Infectious Disease at CDC and he developed, directed and managed the advanced media training for CDC physicians. Bob is a contributing author to the public health textbook: *Principles and Practices of Public Health Surveillance.*

Dave Kuhn conducts law enforcement and first responder training, including terrorism incident response, Miami-Dade, Florida; Dave is also a special advisory member to a Metropolitan Medical Response System (MMRS) and contributor to *Jane's Unconventional Weapons Response Handbook* and *Workplace Security Handbook.*

Fred W. Naeher has over 9 years teaching experience and 10 years in the emergency management field with the State of Montana as the Training and Exercise Manager for Disaster and Emergency Services. He has a BS in both Education and Psychology. He is advisor and trainer for the Montana Behavioral Institute and for the Helena School District Crisis Response Team. He is currently an assessor cadre member for the National Emergency Management Association's accreditation program.

Cathy Paine – Cathy is an Administrator and School Psychologist in Springfield, Oregon. She helped direct the response and recovery efforts following a Springfield school shooting and serves as a consultant to other communities experiencing school violence. Cathy has published articles for the National School Safety Center, the National Association of School Psychologists and the Columbia University Center for the Advancement of Children's Mental Health.

Margaret Preston – Margaret is a developmental counselor with over 20 years experience helping children deal with the affects of traumatic stress. She has worked with the CDC, with special needs children – including but not limited to those with hemophilia – and at the Children's Hospital of the King's Daughters.

Dr. Jean Silvernail – Dr. Silvernail is a program analyst for the Department of Defense's educational opportunities division.

Dr. Ron Stephens – Dr. Ronald Stephens was named executive director of the National School Safety Center in 1985. In this capacity, Dr. Stephens has served as consultant and frequent speaker for school districts, law enforcement agencies and professional organizations worldwide. He serves as executive editor of the *School Safety News Service*, America's leading school crime prevention newsletter. Dr. Stephens was also lead editor of ***Jane's School Safety Handbook, 1st Edition***. Dr. Stephens holds a California teaching credential, administrative credential and a certificate in school business management. His experience includes service as a teacher, assistant superintendent and school board member. His administrative experience includes serving as Chief School Business Officer and as Vice President of Pepperdine University in Malibu, California. Dr. Stephens received his BS in business administration and an MBA from Pepperdine University. He received his EdD from the University of Southern California.

Paul Viollis is lead editor and author of *Jane's Workplace Security Handbook*. Paul is also Managing Director and Practice Leader of the Security Consulting Practice for Citigate Global Intelligence & Security.

Carol Voorhees is a writer for the US Department of Education and co-author of the Secret Service report on School Safety.

Dawn Walker - Dawn has served as a state exercise officer for the State of South Dakota Emergency Management Agency and is currently working for another state office of homeland security.

IMPORTANT

Jane's Teachers' Safety Guide is designed to assist teachers in preventing, planning for, responding to and recovering from any emergency or crisis that may happen at, near or within schools. As such, it should be used in addition to advice from emergency services as well as other appropriate literature.

This book is based on current research, knowledge and understanding, and to the best of the authors' ability the material is current and valid. While the authors, editors, publishers and *Jane's Information Group* have made reasonable efforts to ensure the accuracy of the information contained herein, they cannot be held responsible for any errors found in this book. The authors, editors, publishers and *Jane's Information Group* do not bear any responsibility or liability for the information contained herein or for any uses to which it may be put.

While reasonable care has been taken in the compilation and editing of this title, it should be recognized that the contents are for information purposes only and do not constitute any guidance to the use of the equipment described herein or its rendering safe. *Jane's Information Group* cannot accept any responsibility for any accident, injury, loss or damage arising from use of this information.

Jane's Public Safety Series

Jane's School Safety Handbook, Second Edition
A comprehensive and practical tool to assist teachers, school administrators and other agencies prepare for, respond to and recover from security incidents in schools.

Jane's Safe Schools Planning Guide for All Hazards
The *Jane's Safe Schools Planning Guide for All Hazards* is an essential reference for school planners tasked with designing, implementing and maintaining a safe school plan. Every school should have an effective, locality specific emergency plan in place - this essential guide helps planners do just that. Provides clear, easy to understand, guidelines on how to prevent, prepare for respond to and recover from emergencies.

Jane's Mass Casualty Handbooks: Hospital and Pre Hospital
The *Jane's Mass Casualty Handbooks* provide essential information for emergency response personnel preparing for, responding to and recovering from mass casualty incidents.

Jane's Chem-Bio Handbook
The 2nd edition of the indispensable chem-bio first-response tool includes new information on pre-incident planning, updated treatment procedures, post-incident recovery and a case study of the 2001 anthrax attacks in the US.

Jane's Unconventional Weapons Response Handbook
Essential information to assist first responders recognize and respond to the terrorist and criminal use of unconventional weapons, including 'dirty bombs,' vehicle bombs and directed energy weapons.

Jane's Workplace Security Handbook

Jane's Workplace Security Handbook provides essential information on planning for, responding to and recovering from security threats and incidents that can affect an organization and its employees.

Jane's Crisis Communications Handbook

Jane's Crisis Communications Handbook outlines how to work with the media to inform, direct and calm the public, employees and stakeholders before, during and after emergencies.

Jane's Facility Security Handbook

Detailed security procedures to protect schools, offices, hospitals, utilities, transport systems, entertainment facilities and special events.

Jane's Citizen's Safety Guide

An all-hazards guide for people of varying needs to make calm, quick and safe decisions about potential threats at home, work, school and in the community. The guide provides easy-to-understand emergency procedures and checklists for before, during and after incidents such as natural disasters, mechanical accidents and human-caused emergencies, including terrorism.

Contact your local Jane's representative for more information or visit www.janes.com

Jane's Consultancy

Customized Security Intelligence and Response for Your Requirements

Jane's prides itself on its globally recognized reputation for independent, impartial, accurate and timely security information and analysis, established through our authoritative publications and services on defense, security and international terrorist and criminal activity.

Building on this expertise, Jane's Consultancy provides targeted, customized and confidential solutions that combine Jane's expertise in both threat assessment and mitigation to meet your specific emergency preparedness, response and recovery requirements.

Jane's Consultancy applies an understanding of the motivations, capabilities and methodologies of potential threats to your region, and creates a tailored, comprehensive and robust response plan to mitigate those threats. Key services include:

- Hazard/threat assessments, including 'red teaming'
- Developing an Emergency Operations Plan
- Developing Incident Management/Command Systems
- Conducting training and exercises, including tabletop and full scenarios

For more information, contact your local Jane's representative or simply visit http://consultancy.janes.com or email: consultancy@janes.com

CONTENTS

NOTES

NOTES

Chapter 1

What do teachers need to know?

1.1 Introduction

Teachers face an increasing number of potential hazards during the school day including school shootings, natural disasters, accidents and terrorism. Since the 1970's, disasters and school violence affecting both students and teachers across the United States – sometimes causing multiple injuries and fatalities – has raised awareness of the need for school safety plans. Unfortunately, teachers are often the first to deal with such instances. Through proper training, prepared teachers can deal with emergencies, save lives and limit any damage.

What can teachers do?

Teachers are involved with students on a daily basis – to the extent that they spend more time with the students than their parents. By noticing changes in students and actively listening to them, teachers have the ability to affect students' lives significantly. Overall, teachers need to be involved in all phases of emergencies – from identifying potential dangers, participating in emergency planning, helping to lead students to safety during emergencies as well as taking part in the classroom recovery efforts.

Jane's Teachers' Safety Guide provides guidance and prepares teachers for handling emergency and crisis situations. These easy-to-use procedures can aid in prevention, preparedness, response and recovery and are consistent with national school safety standards at the school and district-levels. It provides emergency response measures to help teachers deal with a wide range of situations such as school violence, terrorism, natural and human caused disasters/accidents, community spillover and health emergencies. In total, the goal of this guide is to support teachers in the event that they are faced with a situation that calls on them to act as first responders.

Resources
Three additional and comprehensive references on the development and implementation of safe school plans are *Practical Information on Crisis Planning – A Guide for Schools and Communities* by the U.S. Department of Education, *Jane's School Safety Handbook, Second Edition* and *Jane's Safe Schools Planning Guide for All Hazards.* The latter two guides are designed to provide safe school planners with information that fits within the framework of a complete safe schools plan in accordance with the emergency response model established in these publications.

Chapter overview
This guide can help prepare teachers and allow them to prevent incidents so that they can keep education as a primary focus. In turn, this chapter will give an overview of what teachers need to know and pay attention to, discussing the following aspects of school safety:

◆   **Threat awareness:** identifying and being aware of potential dangers

◆ **Emergency preparedness:** participating in emergency planning
◆ **Roles and responsibilities:** understanding staff emergency functions before, during and after incidents

1.1.1 Teachers as first responders

Though teachers are not police, fire or EMS personnel, they may need to serve as first responders. According to its formal definition, **first responders are: personnel who arrive first on the scene of an incident and take action to save lives, protect property and meet basic human needs.** This term has increasingly been broadened in recent years to include bystanders who perform search and rescue, transportation and communication during the incident. In their role, teachers can be the first people to provide valuable help to safeguard the students and other school staff.

As first responders, teachers are the first to deal with both major and minor incidents at school. Teachers who think and act quickly during a crisis can save the lives of students and staff. Thus, they should have the tools to prevent or deal with incidents without initial help from professional responders because in most cases, medical or law enforcement officials will not arrive until minutes or, in rare cases, hours or days after the emergency. The measures listed in this guide are intended to help teachers prepare, react and recover from crises as part of their school's emergency plans.

1.1.2 All hazards approach to school safety

The all hazards approach to school safety is an advanced way of approaching school safety issues. Jane's *School Safety* and *Public Safety* series of publications emphasizes this approach as does the US Department of Education. The all hazards approach to school safety is based on the emergency management model and involves four main areas:

◆   Prevention and mitigation
◆   Preparedness
◆   Response
◆   Recovery

A proper safe schools plan will thoroughly address all four phases in written form and will be custom tailored to the needs, resources and risks inherent to the community and the school system. The plan should not only address a limited range of concerns such as violence and terrorism. Accidents, natural and human-caused disasters and severe weather are also major concerns. This guide addresses all four phases as appropriate for the classroom teacher.

Prevention and mitigation

Prevention measures are efforts to keep incidents from occurring. Common examples include implementing an anti-bullying program and using metal detectors and/or dress codes to prevent school violence. Mitigation measures are designed to minimize the adverse impact from incidents that do occur. For example, anchoring classroom bookshelves can help reduce the risk of earthquake-related injuries or installing automatic defibrillators can help students or staff who encounter a heart stoppage.

Preparedness

Preparedness measures are intended to help school staff and emergency responders handle crisis situations as effectively as possible. Preparedness measures include training in emergency procedures, assembling classroom emergency response kits and using drills and exercises to test emergency operations plans with staff, students and local public safety officials. Emergency operations plans (EOPs) list the roles and responsibilities for all school and district staff as well as local public safety to respond to an incident.

Response

Often, teachers will be directly involved in the execution of an emergency response. Response measures involve having systems in place to ensure that the various agencies and organizations that must cooperate under extreme stress in an actual crisis implement the EOP effectively. Common response systems include integrating the incident command system (ICS) into school system emergency preparedness measures. ICS is a system that public safety officials use to create a decision-making authority and ways to cooperate when more than one agency responds to an incident.

Recovery

Recovery measures are designed to minimize the negative effects of a disaster-related crisis on students, staff, emergency response personnel, the affected school(s) and the community. The recovery goal is to restore a sense of normalcy within the school or school system as quickly as possible. Crisis counseling and classroom recovery activities are ways to help resume normal school life.

1.2 Threat awareness

The best approach to prevent or limit potential harm is for the school to conduct a risk and vulnerability assessment. Using the all hazards approach will ensure that the assessment addresses all forms of potential danger. Each school system should use a systematic approach for risk and vulnerability assessments.

In turn, classroom teachers can significantly enhance the level of school safety by looking for any potential sources of harm in their school day, whether that is in the parking lot, the cafeteria or the classroom. Often, teachers can spot hazards that might not be apparent to administrators and external school safety experts or consultants, particularly since they interact with and know the students the most.

Teachers must look out for everyday dangers and report them to school administrators, such as the following:

Students
◆   Unusual or anti-social student behavior
◆   Procedures for managing large groups of children during

---

lunch hour, school assemblies, emergency drills, or other gatherings, that may be unsafe
◆ Field trip procedures that do not properly control children

Facilities
◆ Unsecured areas of the school building and surrounding areas
◆ Unsafe features of the school building that may need maintenance attention, such as uneven floors, jagged or shear table edges, broken doors, unlit exit signs, etc.
◆ Improperly stored cleaning supplies

School location
◆ Is the school located in a low-lying area prone to flooding?
◆ Is the school located on the coast in a hurricane prone area?
◆ Is the school located near a major fault line?
◆ Is the school located in an area frequently hit by tornadoes?
◆ Is the school located near factories or plants that could house hazardous materials?

Teachers should be careful not to focus solely on the issues raised by media coverage or recent local or national tragedies. For example, while it is important to work to reduce the potential of violence in the classroom, other dangers that may result in accidents, are more common.

Teachers should study their schools' EOP to help with accurately assessing the risks in their classrooms. For example, the teacher's emergency flip chart, a quick guide designed to assist a teacher in a crisis, may remind a teacher that the school is located on or near a fault-line where earthquakes are frequent. This should prompt an evaluation of the physical layout of the classroom that could reveal that there are objects that could fall on a child during an earthquake.

Although the activities mentioned seem overwhelming, many emergencies happen unexpectedly and suddenly. Therefore, it is important for teachers to play a major role in school safety. Ongoing training through school professional development sessions and written resources can serve as a critical part of maintaining a safe learning environment.

1.2.1 Student violence

A primary area of concern for many teachers is the potential for violence. Pre-crisis indicators can aid in identifying potential problems and may eliminate or decrease the probability of a violent act. The following indicators may precede the outbreak of conflict at a school:

Discipline problems
◆   Increasing behavior infractions
◆   Perception of unfairness resulting from disciplinary actions
◆   Increasing presence of weapons on campus
◆   Increase in bullying

- Increase in the number of fights on and near campus
- Increase in incidents of intimidation
- Lack of respect for property rights, exhibited by an increase in vandalism, graffiti, theft or destruction

Community/family issues

- Community or family problems that affect students' behavior, performance or attendance
- Unusually high percentage of parental student withdrawals
- Increasing dropout or suspension rate

Group behavior

- Sudden clustering or segregation of various rival groups
- Increase in incidents of gang related activity
- Disproportionate number of unfamiliar guests showing up at school dances or other special events
- Emergence of student underground newspapers or flyers reflecting dissatisfaction or unrest

Often the best way for teachers to notice these behaviors is by **building trust and being actively involved in students' lives.** Learning about students' personal, family and community experiences can often help to ease students' frustrations that may build up and lead to violent outbursts. See *Chapter 6: How Can Teachers Encourage Students to Help with School Safety?*

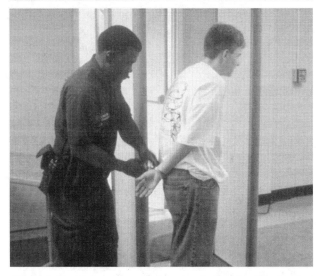

Students that bring weapons to school should not be treated lightly.   **2004**/0564607

It is also important to note that there is no empirically validated way to predict which students will become violent, each of these indicators could signal that violence is more likely to occur. *Chapter 3: Warning Signs: How Can Teachers Spot a Potentially Violent Student* will provide a more in depth assessment of student violence.

1.2.2 Terrorism

Fortunately, government intelligence experts believe that there is a long list of high value targets ahead of schools, such as national landmarks, government buildings and other places of cultural and economic value. While definitions vary, a basic definition of terrorism is the premeditated use/threat of force by non-state actors for political, religious, or ideological purposes. Since the September 11, 2001 terrorist attacks, public concern about domestic vulnerabilities, including schools, has increased dramatically. Despite heightened awareness, terrorist attacks in the United States have so far been relatively rare.

School officials and teachers should be aware that acts of terrorism in the United States and even around the world may negatively affect school children. The death and public outcry often associated with terrorism can be upsetting and can affect the learning environment at a school. In addition, schools with multicultural populations are at a higher risk of incidents of racially charged violence. Students may take out their frustrations on the ethnic population they think is responsible for terrorist attacks.

Schools, however, are not immune to terrorism and are considered 'soft targets' compared with government and military facilities. Soft targets are facilities that do not have high levels of physical security and/or are of secondary interest to terrorist. Terrorists' threat of an attack against a school could exploit the special protectiveness people feel for all children. Terrorists in other countries have not demonstrated restraint in killing children and have even expressly attacked school facilities and school buses. Schools could possibly be targeted or affected by a nearby attack. For example, in the cases of the World Trade Center and Oklahoma City incidents, nearby schools were affected in many ways, from their safety to family reunification.

Unfortunately, some school safety planners have placed too much focus on protecting schools from terrorists and detracted resources from more likely hazards, such as natural or human-caused disasters/accidents, school violence or community spillover.

The all hazards approach to school safety planning can also apply to averting acts of terrorism as with measures to prevent violence in and around the school. For instance, the initial response to a bombing or shooting at a school facility would be the same whether the perpetrators are terrorists or other aggrieved individuals. Teachers, therefore, should be aware of increased terrorist threat warnings as usual but should primarily focus on knowing proper responses to all likely hazards that schools face.

Unrecognized victims of terrorism

Teachers need to be proactive and alert for signs of antagonism toward different ethnic or religious groups in school buildings. An inner city high school in Ohio experienced high levels of tension and dissention weeks after 9/11 between the majority of students and those who appeared to be Muslim or Arab. In some cases, the isolated students were from neither group. Some parents did not allow their children to come to school for weeks because they feared their children would be victims of a backlash.

To remedy this type of situation, teachers need to have open discussions in their classes about the different ethnic groups in their school. Teachers should help students separate the specific act of terrorism from the general ethnic group and emphasize that such individuals at the school most likely have no involvement in terrorism.

1.2.3 Natural disasters

Natural disasters often occur with little or no warning, thus it is imperative that schools prepare teachers, staff and students to respond quickly and appropriately to each situation. Quick and suitable responses can only occur through practice. It is extremely important that teachers participate in drills to ensure that there is a proper response in the classroom.

Drills such as those moving occupants to a tornado safe area within the school or simply lining up at the door in an orderly manner are informal ways to prepare teachers and students to respond before an actual event. If students are not familiar with the response to natural disasters, chaos and panic can quickly develop during an emergency.

Many types of natural disasters affect schools including: fires, tornadoes, severe thunderstorms, hurricanes, floods, earthquakes and severe winter storms. Teachers should be aware of special considerations for each, including how to prevent/mitigate the effects of these hazards and how to respond.

1.2.4 Human-caused disasters/accidents

Human-caused disasters/accidents, like natural disasters, can occur without warning. Many can affect schools, such as transportation accidents, hazardous materials (HazMat) releases, gas leaks and structural failures. Teachers should be aware of special considerations for each, both how to prevent/mitigate the effects of these hazards and how to respond. Teachers can also assist by remaining vigilant in identifying potential problems at the school that could lead to or exacerbate a human-caused disaster or accident.

Although there is usually no forecast for when a human-caused disaster/accident is likely to occur there are identifiable factors, such as:

◆   Proximity to a major highway or known hazardous materials (HazMat) transportation route
◆   Proximity to a chemical facility or nuclear reactor
◆   Structural weaknesses in school facilities

Each school should assess the risks of hazards near their school. Once identified, the school can take measures to mitigate associated risks.

1.2.5 Community spillover

Schools are a reflection of the community. If there are gangs in the community, then it is safe to assume that there are gangs in the school. If a gang related incident occurs outside of school, then retaliation is likely to occur at school. Teachers are an integral part of the notification loop on community incidents, such as gang-related activities. Receiving information about community spillover is important for school safety as it is also a matter of staff workplace security. Teachers should therefore know the climate of the school before entering the building. Setting up lines of communication with the emergency response community will require a great deal of coordination between the school and local law enforcement entities.

1.2.6 Health emergencies

Teachers are front-line personnel in dealing with health emergencies. If students become ill in class or if clusters of students are absent because of illness, teachers need to know that this type of information is important. They should report their observations to the administration to relay to public health officials. Although teachers are not expected to be school nurses, teachers can save lives by doing quick and simple first-aid procedures in the event of a medical emergency. Teachers can also obtain information, such as statistics on seasonal illnesses, that can be used to help prepare their classrooms for expected diseases. For example, teachers can send information home to parents regarding dates of the flu season and ask parents to send extra tissue, antibacterial soap and other supplies for the classroom.

1.3 Emergency preparedness

Although no school can be fully insulated from violence or natural/human-caused disasters, teachers, administrators, law enforcement and emergency management officials can take measures to minimize these threats and create safe campuses. To start this process, school and district officials can create an effective EOP with the following characteristics:

- Includes all hazards and is otherwise comprehensive
- Addresses local risks
- Caters to community resources and needs
- Includes input and assistance from local emergency response professionals

Effective and meaningful EOPs are important for all schools: public/private, elementary/secondary and rural/ suburban/urban. Technological advances, particularly the ability to exchange and share information, enable small rural schools to establish plans equal in scope to those of larger schools. Suburban and rural schools must cope with student fights, weapons, drug abuse and forms of violence once thought to be exclusive to large, urban schools. Private schools have also experienced shootings, edged weapons assaults, hostage situations and other major acts of violence. Private schools are often ill prepared to deal with emergencies as they do not have the same access to transportation and other publicly funded services that require mutual aid agreements with area school districts.

1.3.1 How teachers fit into a safe schools plan

A safe schools plan is a comprehensive plan that school and district officials develop in cooperation with appropriate emergency management officials using an all hazards approach. Teachers are important participants in creating and implementing the safe schools plan because they have a unique perspective of the school due to their direct relationship with students. As previously mentioned, the all hazards safe schools plan has four main elements: prevention, preparedness, response, and recovery. The following are lists of actions that teachers should be aware of which correspond to the different components of an all hazards safe schools plan:

Prevention/Mitigation
♦ Stay alert and report dangerous or suspicious incidents
♦ Pay attention to student behavior. Note sudden and dangerous mood swings.
♦ Report broken fixtures and dangerous areas of school property
♦ Maintain student discipline so that students will listen in an emergency

Preparedness
♦ Attend and play a role at emergency response planning meetings

◆　Make sure that the school conducts preparedness drills
◆　Keep a classroom emergency response kit with updated school information and student release forms

Response

◆　Keep students calm and as safe as possible at all times
◆　Implement appropriate emergency response plan
  ●　Help evacuate students as appropriate during an emergency
  ●　Keep students calm and collected during a lockdown
  ●　Take classroom emergency response kit if directed to evacuate
  ●　Take attendance and account for each child
  ●　Make sure students and staff receive first-aid as necessary
  ●　Manage the release of students after the crisis is brought under control
◆　Give support to school administrators as necessary

Recovery

◆　Work with counselors to restore the mental health of students
◆　Manage relationships with parents and community after an event
◆　Lead and participate in classroom recovery activities
◆　Pay attention to their colleagues and their own recovery

1.3.2 Drilling, training and maintaining readiness

Schools need to conduct drills and exercises to ensure that all school staff (especially teachers) and emergency response personnel understand their roles and that emergency procedures are realistic and are consistent with the emergency management official's procedures. For individual teachers, becoming familiar with emergency procedures and their implementation can significantly enhance performance under stress.

The emergency management community has developed the following types of drills and exercises:

Tabletop exercises ensure emergency management community and teachers know their emergency roles and procedures   **2004**/0564631

◆ **Drills** are normally a single agency exercise to test procedures and allow people to practice critical skills, such as emergency evacuations.

◆ **Tabletop exercises** are typically multi-agency activities conducted in a casual and low stress environment using a pre-scripted written scenario. Participants work through a hypothetical crisis while relying on their instructions in the emergency operations plan.

◆ **Functional exercises** are at first glance much like the tabletop exercise, but tend to be more realistic and high stress. The functional exercises also use pre-scripted scenarios and are normally conducted indoors. The difference is they are run in a real time fashion with streaming messages revealing new information and challenges delivered to participants to add realism and stress.

◆ **Full-scale exercises** are the most realistic type of exercise involving role players who simulate a crisis and response. It is fully simulated and usually conducted in a school building or facility (like a football stadium) or on a school bus. In addition, actual public safety vehicles and equipment are typically used and actions are as realistic as possible. Ordinarily, it is not recommended that students participate in full-scale exercises.

A quality emergency preparedness and response effort will rely on teachers' understanding of policies and procedures and knowing their roles in a crisis. Maintaining preparedness is an ongoing process that involves debriefing following drills and crises, periodic reviews and updates and training. Participants should carry out drills as if an actual event were occurring whether for hostage situations, natural disasters and/or man-made disasters/accident.

1.3.3 Knowing the classroom

Knowing the classroom consists of two main aspects. First, teachers must understand the physical layout of their environment. Second, teachers must understand their students and earn their trust. This is critical for students to listen and follow directions as well as report potentially dangerous situations or students.

Teachers should create a safe environment and develop appropriate procedures to make students feel comfortable reporting incidents of bullying, violence and other serious offenses. Teachers may want to make sure students understand the seriousness of school safety by including school safety topics in lesson plans and class activities.

Classroom environment considerations for teachers

Teachers should be aware of the following considerations about the physical layout of the classroom:

♦ Where are the classroom exits that lead to primary and secondary evacuation routes?
♦ Where is the nearest fire extinguisher and fire alarm?

- Does the classroom have a radio, television, or telephone?
- Are there closets in the classroom that can be locked?
- Where are the light-switches in the classroom?
- Where are the stairwells as well as the elevators?
- Where is the emergency response kit for use during an evacuation? Is it easily accessible? Is it secure? Is it fully stocked with non-expired supplies?
- In a science classroom, where are the emergency showers and eye washes in case of chemical contamination?
- Are dangerous/toxic substances stored in or near the classroom and are they properly secured?
- Is the heating and cooling system protected and behind locked doors?
- Are the lower level windows protected by steel mesh or metal bars?
- Are the parking lots next to the school or under-ground?
- Are all entrances to the school locked?
- Can students climb out of the classroom window during a disaster without causing further harm to themselves?

Teachers should also be aware of the following consider-ations relating to the student population:

Knowledge of the classroom

Teachers and students have survived in emergency situations by using their knowledge of school grounds. A recent shooting at Case Western Reserve University in Cleveland, Ohio, resulted in only one death because the students, teachers and staff, being aware of their surroundings, hid in closets and locked offices as well as under desks and other pieces of furniture. Even though the building had a security monitoring system, an assailant was able to break through a window to gain entry. He held the students and teachers hostage for 5 hours or more.

Source: *The Cleveland Plain Dealer*, May 9, 2003

- ◆ Are there any students in the classroom that do not fit in or exhibit violent or aggressive behavior?
- ◆ Do any students have family problems that may be brought into the classroom?
- ◆ Are there students who have brought weapons into the classroom in the past?

1.4 Roles and responsibilities

Being part of a school community is analogous to being a part of a sports team. Each person has his/her role and covering that position is vital to winning the game. The team is only as strong as the weakest player. The same is true for school safety.

It is a struggle to keep all members of the school community active for a variety of reasons. This includes other teachers, administrators, counselors, psychologists, parents, security guards and supporting public safety agencies. Teachers therefore must follow-up with their counterparts to make sure their reports or concerns are resolved. Teachers are not solely responsible for handling incidents but must play a major role to ensure follow-up occurs quickly and properly.

Not every school district has the exact same roles and responsibilities, but the following can serve as general guidelines.

1.4.1 Teacher

The teacher is responsible for the immediate safety of the classroom and students. This is a very important team position because if the teacher or the students panic, the situation could rapidly deteriorate and lives could be lost. Teachers must establish a level of trust with students and know the emergency plan of the school. Teachers should be aware of their surroundings, question any strangers they see in the building and report incidents or potential dangers.

1.4.2 Principal/administrator/designee

The school Principal **coordinates** the management of the broad areas of school safety:

- Directs school emergency operations plan components
- Activates and oversees the school crisis response team (CRT)

- ◆ Makes decisions about the school day
- ◆ Disseminates information
- ◆ Activates the phone tree if needed
- ◆ Liaises with police, fire and other decision-makers and responders

During an incident

In an incident that impacts an entire school district, the **Superintendent** may assume the crisis coordinator role. It is critical that the Principal not be in charge of more duties than one person can handle. Too often, the Principal is the only person designated to carry out a number of keys tasks. The result is a choke point in the response process when the Principal is overwhelmed.

1.4.3 School crisis response team (CRT)

Schools use different names to refer to the group of trusted, responsible members of administration and teachers who are **trained in responding to a variety of crisis and emergency situations**. This guide refers to this group as the crisis response team (CRT) for continuity. The CRT responds to varying levels of crises on a daily basis. When the level of crisis requires police/fire response, the CRT members become **component leaders** under the emergency operations plan.

1.4.4 Planning committee

A safe schools planning committee, comprised of school administrators, teachers and parents, should meet on **an**

ongoing basis to develop and **revise** the EOP. The planning committee should provide the following functions:

◆ Maintain staff awareness of disaster threats

◆ Conduct drills and exercises – that are properly designed and evaluated – as well as arrange or conduct training

◆ Inventory staff members to determine skills that may be useful in disaster planning, such as first aid, CPR certification, bilingual capabilities, HAM radio operation ability

◆ Equip the command post area which serves as the base of operations to manage an incident. It should contain a floor plan of the school, a current personnel roster, critical telephone numbers and a dependable communications system.

◆ Designate a media spokesperson and a communications team

◆ Develop a release plan for employees. It should take into account family and other responsibilities outside the workplace.

◆ Promote employee family preparedness

◆ Promote student family preparedness

◆ Encourage staff to keep an emergency kit with supplies, such as food, water, flashlight, medication and sturdy shoes, in a safe, accessible place

1.4.5 Incident command system

In many instances, the response to an emergency will require the use of the incident command system (ICS). Teachers must be familiar with this system of crisis management and be prepared to work within ICS. As a teacher, understanding how these agencies work together and with the school's response plan is very important to respond to emergencies in a coordinated and effective manner. If possible, teachers should take the following measures before an emergency:

◆ Attend training on ICS
◆ Know the school's emergency response plan to specific incidents
◆ Attend community drills and exercises

1.4.6 Incident command post

During an active crisis, public safety officials and the school system will establish an incident command post (CP) from which to coordinate a response. Representatives from different emergency response agencies, the school district and effected school(s) will be present to serve as a direct link with the affected agencies. The CP ensures that the appropriate emergency response plan is enacted. **Critical decision-makers should staff the CP** and may include: school Superintendent, Principal, Police Chief, Fire Chief, hospital administrator, City Manager and their respective Public Information Officers.

1.4.7 School administrators and staff

School administrators and staff are responsible for the **safety of students** in their care and control. They are not (nor are teachers) expected to face down a gunman, handle a bomb or take a knife away from someone. They will either safely secure the students and employees or evacuate the students and employees while the police and/or fire department handle the incident. However, schools must be prepared to assist public safety officials and plan how to administer this assistance.

1.4.8 School resource officer or first officer on the scene

Under ICS, in a criminal situation the first officer on the scene, on many occasions the school resource officer, will be in charge of the situation until a higher ranking law enforcement officer assumes control of the scene.

Having law enforcement officers in the building each day is usually a sufficient deterrent to violence. When this is not the case, the school must rely on outside agencies to come to their aid. In the meantime, everyone in the building must be serious and calm.

1.4.9 Police

The police are **in charge** of an incident when a crime is involved. They will set up an on-scene incident command post (CP). School administrators and staff will **support the police** in obtaining information regarding students, facility layout, moving students, etc.

1.4.10 Fire department

The fire department is in charge when a fire or other non-criminal, life-threatening emergency occurs. In most com-

The fire department is in charge during fires and other non-criminal, life-threatening emergencies   **2003**/0562459

munities, the fire services are also the lead agency for rescue operations, with support from law enforcement, emergency management and emergency medical service personnel.

1.4.11 Emergency management personnel

Emergency management personnel are typically the most qualified to assist with emergency operations planning, design, coordination and evaluation of drills and exercises. They also help to coordinate response and recovery efforts. They typically serve as the hub agency to ensure that other agencies can smoothly work together.

1.4.12 Emergency medical personnel

Field responders, such as paramedics and hospital emergency room staff, are key players in planning and preparing for major incidents as well as for incident responses. They are of particular importance in mass casualty incidents.

1.4.13 Public health officials

Public health officials are particularly helpful in dealing with a range of situations including mass contamination incidents from tainted food, natural or human-caused outbreaks of disease such as a bio-terrorism incident.

1.5 Conclusion

Teachers play an important part in school safety. No one expects or desires teachers to play 'hero' by putting themselves in harm's way. Teachers who know their classrooms and their crisis response roles and responsibilities can be prepared to help keep the students and themselves safe.

Sources:
Tom Breckenridge, "Frightened faculty, students hid in locked offices," Cleveland Plain Dealer, 05/10/03.
Practical Information on Crisis Planning – A Guide for Schools and Communities, U.S. Department of Education

NOTES

NOTES

Chapter 2

Teacher safety – how do teachers minimize risk and prepare for incidents?

2.1 Introduction

To maintain an effective learning environment for students, teachers must think about how to limit potential disturbances in the classroom before they appear. Introducing strategies to reduce risk from dangers (often called prevention/mitigation) is essential for the safety of students as well as teachers. In addition, planning and preparation can aid teachers who must respond to emergencies. The guidelines in this chapter are intended to aid teachers in preventing crises before they occur and preparing for those crises that cannot be prevented. Teachers should refer to the school's emergency operations plans for further direction on what prevention measures they can take.

Chapter overview
This chapter is intended to aid teachers in:

♦   Identifying threats and taking prevention measures
♦   Maintaining physical safety and reducing risk
♦   Preparing for incidents that cannot be prevented

2.2 Threats to teachers

Teachers are now confronted with a classroom environment more dangerous than only a few years ago. Very few teacher training programs, however, address how to deal with the wide variety of threats in the classroom. Violence, including crimes against teachers, in both rural and urban schools can potentially endanger the lives of those tasked with instructing our youth. Immediate concerns about terrorism within the U.S. have made teachers more aware of the potential impact to schools. Teachers continue to deal with natural and human-caused disasters that are much more common, yet unpreventable. Teachers are also painfully aware of the spillover effects from the surrounding community, such as gang violence and drug use, on the classroom. This section will address each of these threats to give teachers a better understanding of how to handle potentially harmful classroom situations.

2.2.1 Crimes against teachers

School violence and crime can affect anyone at a school, creating a high-stress and hostile learning or working environment. While the media may focus on students, teachers are also common victims of nonfatal crimes. According to a joint study published by the U.S. Departments of Education and Justice, from 1997 to 2001, approximately 1.3 million nonfatal crimes were committed against teachers. Crimes "at school" happened inside a school building, on school property, or at a work site.

Most crimes against teachers involve theft. In the same 5-year period, teachers were the victims of an average of 817,000 thefts and 473,000 violent crimes. Violent crimes included rape, sexual assault, robbery, and aggravated assault. This translates into an annual rate of 21 violent crimes and 37 thefts for every 1,000 teachers.

Teachers in urban schools are more vulnerable than others to crime at school. Teachers in urban schools were more likely to be the victims of violent crimes (28 out of every 1,000 teachers) than were teachers in suburban or rural schools (13 and 16, respectively, out of every 1,000).

Sometimes offenses are committed by students who verbally threaten or physically attack teachers. In the 1999-2000 school year, 305,000 teachers were victims of threats of injury by students and 135,000 were victims of attacks by students. Generally, public school teachers (10 percent) were more prone to threats than private school teachers (4 percent).

These statistics send the message that teachers must be aware of their safety and physical surroundings. Incidents and crises affect teachers just as much as students.

Source: Indicators of School Crime and Safety: 2003, Departments of Education and Justice, Sixth edition, October 2003

2.2.2 School violence: what teachers need to know

Student violence has received the most media attention out of all threats in the classroom. Although these attacks are less common than other threats to the school, the prospect of a student using a weapon in the classroom can be terrifying. Fortunately, many incidents of school violence can be prevented. Teachers and school administrators are most likely to deal with violent students before emergency personnel can arrive because of the generally short duration of such incidents. It is thus extremely important for teachers to prepare for these contingencies.

The following statistics obtained from several reports sourced below should give teachers a sense of the threats they may face from student violence:

Are schools becoming more violent?

◆ In 1998, 65 percent of public school teachers and 60 percent of students report that the level of violence in their school had stayed the same within the past year; 21 percent of teachers and 29 percent of students report that the level of violence had decreased; 23 percent of teachers and 28 percent of students report that violence is likely to increase in the next two years

How safe is my school?

◆ 75 percent of public school teachers feel very safe when they are at school
◆ 56 percent of public school students feel very safe at school

How likely am I to be a victim of violence at school?

◆ In 1998, 16 percent of public school teachers have been a victim of violence. This has risen from 11 percent of school teachers in 1993.
◆ 24 percent of public school students have been the victim of violence
◆ 37 percent of public school students have pushed, shoved, grabbed or slapped someone else

Are weapons prevalent in my school?

◆ Two percent of public school students have used a knife or fired a gun at school

◆ Public school teachers report that 0.8 percent of students regularly carry weapons such as handguns or knives to school

◆ 12 percent of public school students report that they have carried a weapon to school at some point

◆ Less than one percent of juveniles between the ages of 12 and 16 reported that they carried a handgun on school property within the past month in 1997

◆ In 1997, 9 percent of high school students reported that they carried a weapon on school property in the past month

When do violent incidents happen?

◆ In 1997, violent incidents by juveniles between the ages of 12 and 16 peaked in the afternoon around 3:00pm at the end of the school day.

How are on-campus weapons discoveries addressed?

◆ 3,657 students were expelled from school in the 2000–2001 school year for bringing a firearm to school

◆ 47 percent of expulsions for bringing a firearm to school involved high school students; 28 percent were middle school students and 24 percent were elementary-school aged students in 2000–2001 school year

Sources:
Metropolitan Life Insurance Company, *The Metropolitan Life Survey Of The American Teacher: Violence In America's Public Schools – Five Years Later*. NY, NY, 1999.

Howard N. Snyder, Melissa Sickmund, *Juvenile Offender and Victims 1999 National Report*, National Center for Juvenile Justice, 1999.

U.S. Department of Education, *Report on the Implementation of the Gun-Free Schools Act in the States and Outlying Areas: School Year 2000–2001*, October 2003.

Teacher actions points: prevent/mitigate school violence

Schools can make the best use of their resources by focusing on **prevention** rather than relying on law enforcement to respond and resolve violent incidents after they happen. As "first responders" and students' initial point of contact, teachers are on the front line of prevention efforts.

- ◆ **Use good judgment**. A teacher's most important resource in any potentially violent situation is his/her good judgment. Reacting to potential violence in the classroom can keep a minor behavioral infraction from escalating and appropriately resolve the violent situation.
- ◆ **Listen**. Teachers should listen to students about their hardships and any potential confrontation. Many rumors of confrontations are false, but asking questions and

Guns can be brought into schools using disguises like book bags, purses or sporting equipment
Source: Safe Havens International   **2004**/0564670

following up on these bits of information could save lives.

◆   **Gather information**. Teachers and the school administration should make an effort to gather information from the friends and classmates of students at risk of becoming violent. In many cases, students hear of potential violence before it occurs.

◆   **Alert the Principal**. Information that teachers gather and report to the Principal or other school officials can successfully thwart potential crises. The Principal will enact proper response protocols and deal with the issue accordingly.

- **Be careful of items used to disguise weapons**. Schools can take a step against violence by prohibiting book bags in the classroom. Weapons are more easily concealed in book bags than notebooks. Large purses can also present a problem.

- **If practical, leave classroom doors open and windows uncovered**. If a dangerous situation develops in the classroom, a passing teacher or student can alert someone else in the building to provide assistance.

Despite the best efforts of teachers, violence may still occur in the classroom. Teachers should have some idea about how to best prevent damage or injuries to themselves and their students.

2.2.3 Terrorism

What teachers need to know about terrorism
Domestic incidents of terrorism, although rare, can also cause high levels of anxiety. Teachers with no control over the incidence of terrorism can feel helpless and panic. Teachers do not necessarily need to understand the terrorists' goals or motivations when planning to mitigate the impact of attacks, however. Also, teachers and school administrators may have no idea in the immediate aftermath of an incident if it was perpetrated by terrorists. If biological agents or contaminants are used, teachers may have to prepare themselves for dealing with an incident where signs and symptoms may not appear for some time afterwards.

Teacher action points: prevent/mitigate the impact of terrorism

◆ **Read and understand the school's emergency operations plan and emergency response plans**. Certain procedures such as bomb threats, hostage situations, and shootings can be considered acts of terrorism. No matter the perpetrator, the response should be in accordance with the school's plans.

◆ **Understand the implications of anniversary dates**. Sometimes, a violent incident is planned around significant anniversary dates that are either historical in nature, as was the Oklahoma City bombing, or a date of a previous large-scale crisis.

◆ **Be alert and aware of surroundings**. Teachers should know the proper reporting procedures for suspicious persons in and around the school.

◆ **Be aware and cognizant of the various levels of the national Homeland Security Advisory System**. It is important to understand how each will affect the safety of the community and school

Preparation

Building upon this last suggestion, it is advisable for teachers to become familiar with the meaning of each threat condition and take actions as appropriate to implement the recommendations. Below is a guide for schools to follow alerts for each threat condition.

Color coded threat levels help communicate overall risk

Low condition (Green)

DHS declares a **Low Condition** when there is perceived to be a low risk of terrorist attacks. Under this condition, DHS advises federal, state and local departments and agencies to consider the following:

- Refine and exercise preplanned protective measures as appropriate
- Ensure personnel receive proper training on the Homeland Security Advisory System and specific

preplanned department or agency protective measures
- Institutionalize a process to ensure that all facilities and regulated sectors are regularly assessed for vulnerabilities to terrorist attacks and all reasonable measures are taken to mitigate these vulnerabilities
- Train all crisis response team (CRT) personnel; drill students on evacuations (i.e. bomb threat evacuation)
- Restock emergency response kits and other emergency kits
- Review and revise school plans and classroom emergency procedures with students as appropriate

Guarded condition (Blue)

DHS declares a **Guarded Condition** when a general risk of terrorist attacks is perceived. In addition to the protective measures taken in the Low (Green) Condition, DHS advises federal, state, and local departments and agencies to consider the following general measures in addition to any agency specific protective measures:

- Check communications with designated emergency response or command locations
- Review and update emergency response procedures
- Provide the public and parents with any information that would strengthen their ability to act appropriately
- Conduct call-downs (calling CRT members using a calling tree or other type of phone list) and alerts with proper CRT members as well as with the school system's district office

◆ Practice classroom lockdown procedures with students
◆ Ensure that visitor sign-in procedures are current and enforced by all staff

Elevated condition (Yellow)

DHS declares an **Elevated Condition** when a significant risk of terrorist attacks is perceived. In addition to the protective measures taken in the previous threat conditions, DHS advises federal, state and local departments and agencies to consider the following general measures in addition to the agency specific protective measures:

◆ Increase surveillance of critical locations (playgrounds, athletic fields, etc.)
◆ Coordinate emergency plans as appropriate with nearby jurisdictions and public safety agencies
◆ Assess whether the precise characteristics of the threat require the further refinement of preplanned protective measures
◆ Implement as appropriate, contingency and emergency response plans
◆ Review roles and responsibilities of school response personnel
◆ Provide refresher courses/workshops for CRT members

High condition (Orange)

DHS declares a **High Condition** when it perceives a high risk of terrorist attacks. In addition to the protective measures taken in the previous threat conditions, DHS advises federal, state and local departments and agencies to consider the following general measures in addition to the agency specific protective measures:

♦ Coordinate necessary security efforts with federal, state, and local law enforcement agencies or National Guard or other appropriate armed forces organizations. Schools will also coordinate efforts with neighboring schools and districts.

♦ Take additional precautions at school events and possibly consider alternative venues or even cancellation

♦ Prepare to execute contingency procedures, such as moving to an alternate site or dispersing the student body

♦ Restrict facility access to essential personnel only and ensure that visitor sign-in procedures are strictly enforced

♦ Schools should also consider implementing a partial lockdown, which requires simply locking the outside doors to restrict access into the building except by the front door

Severe condition (Red)

DHS declares a **Severe Condition** when a severe risk of terrorist attacks is perceived. Under most circumstances, the protective measures for a **Severe Condition** are not intended to be sustained for substantial periods of time. In addition to the protective measures in the previous threat conditions, DHS recommends federal, state and local departments and agencies to consider the following general measures in addition to the agency specific protective measures:

◆ Increase or redirect personnel to address critical emergency needs
◆ Assign emergency response personnel and pre-position and mobilize specially trained teams or resources
◆ Monitor, redirect, or constrain transportation systems
◆ Implement the emergency operation and response plans
◆ Activate the appropriate CRTs
◆ Close public and government facilities, including schools

Source: U.S. Department of Homeland Security and Georgia Emergency Management Agency (GEMA)

2.2.4 Natural disasters

Though there is no way to prevent the onset of a natural disaster, teachers have been preparing classrooms for natural disasters, such as tornadoes, for many decades. These events, though unpreventable, are somewhat predictable. Effective procedures can be set in place to mitigate potential damage and keep students and teachers safe.

Teachers action points: preparing for natural disasters

Teachers should take the following actions to help prevent/ mitigate the impact of natural disasters:

◆ Learn the type of natural disasters that pose the greatest hazards in the community. Many of these hazards should be listed in the school's all hazards plan.

- Monitor local emergency broadcast stations in the event of a natural disaster to obtain the most up-to-date information about the event. If the school has weather radio, it is important that teachers know where the radio is located.

- Know the policies for school cancellations and closings in order to help disseminate this information to parents and students

- If necessary, work with school maintenance personnel to obtain the necessary materials and information about boarding-up classroom windows

- Learn the differences between a severe weather "Watch" (when an event may happen) and "Warning" (when an event is very likely to happen or is happening). Each notification has unique implications.

- Know where protected areas are located within the school

- Display posters in the classroom alerting students of "safe areas" so students can visualize daily where they will need to go in the event of a natural disaster. This is also helpful in case the regular teacher is absent the day of disaster.

- Prepare students for the seriousness of natural disasters by conducting drills, providing discussion time, showing actual film footage of disasters and having occasional speakers in the classroom from the emergency management community.

- Keep a ready reference flip-chart that succinctly explains all possible emergency procedures in every classroom. This can be in the form of a small hand-held, portable chart or a large chart for everyone to see.

The following are steps for teachers to remember to help mitigate the impact of each type of natural disaster the school may face.

Fire

◆ Know where fire-extinguishers and fire-alarms are located

◆ Know primary and secondary evacuation routes as well as primary and secondary evacuation meet-up sites

◆ Make sure schools test fire alarms regularly to ensure they are working properly

◆ Look around for fire hazards like excessive clutter, unsafe wiring, exposed hazardous material containers, etc.

◆ Hold regular fire drills and make sure students know the location of fire extinguishers, alarms, evacuation routes and meet-up sites

◆ Prepare an emergency response kit to take in case of evacuation; have it in an easily accessible, yet secure, location

Severe thunderstorm

◆ Know the location of "safe-areas," such as basements or internal rooms without windows, in case weather becomes very severe

◆ Pay attention to announcements relayed on radio or television, or by the front office of the school

◆ Prepare an emergency response kit to take in case of

evacuation and have it in an easily accessible, yet secure, location

♦ Have a plan for rapidly moving students indoors if severe weather threatens

Tornado

♦ Know the difference between a Tornado Watch (when a tornado is likely) and a Tornado Warning (when a tornado has been spotted or is approaching)

♦ Pay attention to announcements of a Tornado Watch or Warning relayed on radio or television, or by the front office of the school

♦ Know the location of "safe-areas," such as basements or internal rooms without windows, in case a Tornado Warning is issued

♦ If the plan calls for remaining in school room, practice **"drop, cover and hold" drills with students**
   ● Drop below a sturdy desk or table
   ● Hold on
   ● Protect eyes by pressing face against arms

♦ Pay attention to announcements relayed on radio or television, or by the front office of the school

♦ Prepare an emergency response kit to take in case of evacuation and have it in an easily accessible, yet secure, location

♦ Hold regular tornado drills and make sure students pay attention to the location of "safe-areas"

Teachers can learn the natural disasters that pose the greatest risk in their communities   **2003**/0564503

◆ Have a plan for rapidly moving students indoors if severe weather threatens

Hurricane
◆ Know the difference between a Hurricane Watch (when a hurricane is moving toward land and has the potential to cause hurricane conditions on the coast within 48 hours) and a Hurricane Warning (when hurricane conditions are expected within 24 hours)
◆ Prepare an emergency response kit to take in case of evacuation and have it in an easily accessible, yet secure, location
◆ Prepare for potential power failures due to high wind

- Stay abreast of hurricane tracking information and forcasts via weather radio, television or the internet
- Know the location of "safe-areas," such as second story rooms or internal rooms without windows in case a Hurricane Warning is issued
- Familiarize yourself with hurricane evacuation routes
- Prepare for the eventuality that the school may be used as a hurricane shelter if it is located on high ground a reasonable distance from the coastline
- Follow any school protection instructions such as taping windows or removing debris from the school yard

Flood

- Know the difference between a Flood or a Flash Flood Watch (flooding is possible in the area) and a Flood or a Flash Flood Warning (flooding is occurring or is expected to occur in the area)
- Know the school's emergency response plan in case of a flood, if evacuation is necessary or if the school is on high ground
- Prepare an emergency response kit to take in case of evacuation and have in an easily accessible, yet secure, location
- Prepare to evacuate to higher ground if the school is in the flood zone
- Know the local flood evacuation routes
- Prepare for the eventuality that the school may be used as a flood shelter

Earthquake

- Make sure shelves are fastened securely to the wall
- Place large or heavy objects on the ground or on lower shelves
- Make sure overhead light fittings are secure
- Practice **"drop, cover and hold"** drills with students
  - Drop next to a sturdy desk or table
  - Hold on
  - Protect eyes by pressing face against arms
  - If no table or desk is nearby, sit on the floor against an interior wall away from windows, bookcases or other objects that could fall
- Identify **safe places in every room**, for example:
  - Strong furniture (heavy desk/table)
  - Against an inside wall
  - Away from windows or anywhere with glass that might shatter (pictures, mirrors and so on)
- Prepare an emergency response kit to take in case of evacuation and have it in an easily accessible, yet secure, location

Severe winter storm

- In case the electricity is cut off, make sure that the classroom has sufficient supplies to keep students warm, such as blankets
- Make sure students bring heavy coats to school if a major storm is a possibility
- Prepare activities that will keep children from going outside

◆   Have emergency response kit readily accessable

Severe heat wave

◆   Make sure students wear weather appropriate clothing
     (i.e. lightweight and light colored clothing)
◆   Give students plenty of water breaks if they are outside
◆   Know the signs of heat stroke
    ●   Cessation of perspiration
    ●   Overheating
    ●   Dizziness/Weakness
    ●   Rapid pulse
    ●   Nausea
◆   Limit any heavy exertion under heat wave conditions

Source: **Jane's Citizen's Safety Guide**

2.2.5 Human-caused disasters/accidents

Human-caused disasters/accidents in some situations can be
prevented. Teachers should be alert for unsafe placement of
potentially hazardous items or needed maintenance on school
grounds that could cause accidents if left unchanged. It will
be helpful to have knowledge of safety audit and site survey
results that schools may maintain. Also, familiarization with
evacuation routes, staging areas and crisis response teams
(CRTs) will undoubtedly help teachers understand how and
where to seek help if needed.

Teacher action points: prevent/mitigate man-made disasters and accidents

- Understand the school's policies and procedures on conducting safe evacuations.
- Be familiar with carrying out the school's functional protocols.
- Remember, a teacher's primary responsibility is the safety and accountability for all students.
- Teachers should understand their responsibilities in the event of an emergency

Transportation accident

- Keep information on students' modes of transportation (bus riders, car riders, walkers, etc.)
- Ensure that information on chaperones and any other staff that accompanies a field trip is collected

Hazardous material (HazMat) release

- Know primary and secondary evacuation routes as well as primary and secondary evacuation meet-up sites for this type of emergency
- Prepare an emergency response kit to take in case of evacuation and have in an easily accessible, yet secure, location
- Know the appropriate shelter-in-place procedures for your school in the event of a hazmat incident
- Know the appropriate evacuation procedures in the event that you must evacuate
- Have a system in place for keeping account of all students

Gas leak

♦ Know primary and secondary evacuation routes as well as primary and secondary evacuation meet-up sites for this type of emergency

♦ Prepare an emergency response kit to take in case of evacuation and have it in an easily accessible, yet secure, location

♦ Know the appropriate evacuation procedures in the event of a gas leak

♦ Have a system in place for keeping account of all students

Structural failure

♦ Know primary and secondary evacuation routes as well as primary and secondary evacuation meet-up sites for this type of emergency

♦ Prepare an emergency response kit to take in case of evacuation and have it in an easily accessible, yet secure, location

♦ Know the appropriate evacuation procedures in the event of structural failure

♦ Have a system in place for keeping account of all students

Chemical/biological/radiological/nuclear (CBRN) attack

♦ Know the appropriate duck and cover procedures in the event of a CBRN related explosion

♦ Know the appropriate shelter-in-place procedures

♦ Know the appropriate evacuation procedures

- Familiarize yourself with evacuation routes
- Familiarize yourself with personal decontamination procedures (see *Chapter 4 section 4.15.3*)
- Prepare an emergency response kit to take in case of evacuation and have it in an easily accessible, yet secure, location

Power outage

- Make sure the emergency response kit contains a flashlight and extra batteries
- Take extra precautions if anticipating severe hot or cold weather

2.2.6 Community spillover

Teachers should be aware that problems in communities in which students live are not left at the classroom door. Gang rivalries, drug use, and theft can impact the safety of students and teachers. Teachers have a very real interest in mitigating the effects of these conflicts in the classroom. Allowing time to discuss neighborhood problems could help to defuse situations or bring to light information that can be passed on to the police.

Teachers action points: prevent/mitigate and prepare for community spillover

- Be aware of the warning signs such as excessive fighting, severe rage, gang hand signs, gang paraphernalia, etc. Any should be noted and reported to school administrators.

- Know how to report untoward and destructive behavior. Obtain proper classroom intervention information from the school resource officer (SRO) and school mental health personnel.
- Understand the use of emergency codes and procedures and the school's policies on who can initiate these procedures if necessary
- Talk to students about the consequences of unacceptable behavior
- Preplan action steps of how to report fights and other conflicts in the classroom. Ask the SRO for specific techniques and ideas on how to quickly deescalate conflicts. Practice the action steps and participate in school exercises and drills.

School Resource Officers can identify ways to prevent/ mitigate and prepare for community spillover into the classrooms
Source: Safe Havens International   **2004**/0564669

2.3 Physical safety

Remember that first and foremost, teacher safety is paramount. No matter the type of situation, teachers should maintain their personal safety at all times. Unfortunately, experience has demonstrated that teachers are sometimes victims of theft and even acts of violence while working. As with many other professions, educators should utilize prevention techniques tailored to their unique work environment. While not every measure is appropriate for every situation, the following recommendations are concepts which generally serve to reduce risk when applied appropriately and consistently:

Prevent theft
◆ Keep personal property locked up at all times
◆ Do not leave belongings unattended
◆ Mark valuables with ID

Leaving work and staying late
◆ When leaving the school building, have keys in hand for fast entry into your vehicle
◆ Notify the administrator in charge if staying late
◆ When staying late, park vehicle in a well-lighted area
◆ If leaving school late, call someone before leaving; do not walk to parked vehicles alone.

School safety programs

◆ Learn how to prevent crimes by attending programs offered to the staff and faculty by school system's school safety and security department

◆ Inquire whether the school has a highly visible and interactive presence by the school resource officer who deals with law enforcement

Other proactive steps

◆ Inventory your campus to identify safe and unsafe areas in and around the school. Make suggestions of strategies for modifying those unsafe areas

◆ Insist that administrators enforce the student code of conduct

◆ Be sure to keep administrators informed of any repeated problems with specific students

◆ Report to the administration any rumors or comments overheard about impending violence

◆ If assaulted, **press charges**. Also, take the leave time offered by the school district

◆ Know the state laws for school safety

2.4 Conclusion

In conclusion, threats to teachers, practices for reducing risks during natural or human-caused disasters and physical safety are issues that it is helpful for teachers to face and discuss Teachers who continue to seek training and education concerning all aspects of safety issues can further improve their ability to reduce risk in schools.

NOTES

NOTES

Chapter 3

Recognizing warning signs – how can teachers spot a potentially violent student?

3.1 Introduction

Teachers can make a difference in preventing and reducing school violence by remaining aware of signs that may precede it. After reviewing past incidents of school violence, psychologists and police investigators have identified common warning signs that violent students have demonstrated. While these warning signs show some consistency, no formula can accurately predict violent behavior. Several federal government studies have revealed that the numerous differences between the student offenders in planned school shootings make 'profiling' unreliable. Therefore, in order to intervene or prevent potentially fatal incidents, **teachers must consider all available information in context with the situation, the students involved, past incidents and the school safety environment.**

Chapter overview

This chapter provides teachers with background and guidance on dealing with warning signs that can lead to school violence, including the following:

- Types of school violence
- Trends and common aspects in shooting incidents
- Behaviors that can precede violence
- Lower-level violent incidents that can precede larger-scale violence
- Teacher action points to intervene and/or prevent violence
- Procedures on reporting incidents

NOTE: In all instances of intervention, teachers should seek the support and input of the school administration when pursuing any options. Promote a multi-faceted approach with open lines of communication with key colleagues: assistant principals, department heads, counselors, psychologists, school resource officers, security guards and students (when appropriate).

3.2 Types of school violence

Most incidents of school violence do not involve fatalities or multiple victims and do not receive widespread media coverage, if any. For example, there have been 350 known incidents of school-associated violent deaths in the United States since 1992 according to the National School Safety Center (NSSC) report *School Associated Violent Deaths* (2003). Although any death is tragic, this number is small compared to the 53.6 million students in around 119,000 primary and secondary schools in 2002 alone, according the National Center for Education Statistics. According to the *1999 Annual Report on School Safety*, the risk for students suffering a violent death in school is also low – less than one in one million. Fortunately, most of the strategies that reduce the risk of school shootings can help reduce the incidence of all types of violence on campus.

Most student violence takes the form of **low-level pushing and shoving**. Unfortunately, students can unintentionally escalate these incidents into major fights and even the use of weapons. Student aggravated assault and even homicide often result from seemingly trivial matters between young people who know each other. Such minor incidents would have otherwise culminated in less serious offenses had an intervention occurred.

Types of violence other than targeted school shootings that can affect the school include the following:

- Bullying
- Fights
  - Gang-related
  - Drug-related
- Domestic violence
  - Child abuse
  - Spousal abuse/abusive relationships
- Interpersonal problems between students
- Vandalism
- Theft
- Area crime

3.2.1 Student rationale for physical violence

Many young people think it is natural, almost required, behavior to seem "cool" by play fighting, pushing, shoving or pretending to face off with another student at or near the school. A student's violent behavior does not stem from a lack of values. Rather, it is grounded in a well-developed code that holds such behavior to be a justifiable, commonsense way to achieve certain goals. Many students find it essential to maintain a "tough" image. In turn, it is hard for many students to "lose face" by failing to defend him or herself, a friend or a loved one through violence. Some individuals join groups or gangs that can contribute to the escalation of violence.

Combined, the trend of lower-level physical violence, fed by a prideful student mentality, suggests that educators should focus more on preventing or reporting routine acts of school violence to reduce potential escalation that can involve rare acts of lethal violence.

Source: Daniel Lockwood, "Violence Among Middle School and High School Students," National Institute of Justice, October 1997.

3.3 Research on violent youth

School officials, psychologists, law enforcement and youth service professionals have conducted extensive research to establish a set of criteria that can help predict violent offenders in schools. Since the early 1990s, the National School Safety Center (NSSC), the U.S. Department of Education, the Federal Bureau of Investigation (FBI), the U.S. Secret Service and the Centers for Disease Control and Prevention (CDC) have conducted various studies to identify predictive factors of school violence. Each study has helped to increase the understanding of violent behavior and its implications for teachers, school administrators and law enforcement officials as they attempt to prevent and respond to such risks.

3.3.1 Trends in shooting incidents

Studies have tracked commonalities among violent incidents involving firearms. A study appearing in the *Journal of the American Medical Association* concluded the following regarding student attackers in school shooting incidents from 1994–1999:

◆ **Demographic:** 95 percent were male
◆ **Previous offenses:**
  ● 47 percent of attackers had been criminally charged for other offenses
  ● 40 percent were members of a gang
  ● 37 percent had been reported for fighting peers
  ● 29 percent had been reported for disobedience
◆ **Previous victimization:** 20 percent were bullied by peers
◆ **Substance use:** 4 percent were under the influence of alcohol or drugs at the time of the shooting

Source: Anderson et al, "School Associated Violent Deaths in the United States, 1994–1999," Journal of the American Medical Association, Vol. 286, No. 21, December 5, 2001.

With the available data, it is difficult to go beyond general percentages and accurately predict violent youth behavior. Researchers have concluded that **there is no way to identify dangerous students who may harm themselves or others accurately.**

Nevertheless, learning about common characteristics may help teachers understand and notice a student's potential for harming themselves or others **in the context of the entire school environment**. This may also help teachers take appropriate action if necessary. Therefore, teachers who spend the time and effort to know more about their students can make a difference, particularly in reducing the incidence of violence.

3.3.2 Common elements of school shootings

The Secret Service/Department of Education's *Final Report and Findings of the Safe School Initiative* released in 2002 and the FBI's *The School Shooter: A Threat Assessment Perspective* released in 2000 have both been instrumental in defining some common characteristics related to incidents of school-associated violence.

The report by the Secret Service and the Department of Education focused on "targeted violence" – incidents in which a known (or probable) attacker targeted an identified (or identifiable) person, building or school. The study included 37 school shootings that were clearly unrelated to gang or drug activity. The study also did not include shootings related to interpersonal or relationship problems. The following conditions were the most common which teachers can address through preventive strategies:

- ◆ Shooters made plans ahead of time
- ◆ Other people knew ahead of time

- The shooter previously used weapons
- There is no uniform profile
- Bystanders resolved the incident before authorities arrived
- Other students were involved

See: *Section 3.6 Teacher action points to prevent school violence.*

Shooters made plans ahead of time

The shooters included in the Secret Service/Department of Education survey did not come to school and merely open fire without warning. There was an identifiable progression of activities leading up to the incident. In 95 percent of incidents, the shooters developed the idea to harm someone else at least two weeks in advance and planned the shooting more than two days in advance. The perpetrators of the Columbine High School attack planned their assault for more than two years.

Other people knew ahead of time

In 81 percent of all incidents included in the Secret Service/Department of Education study, the shooter told someone else of their intentions to harm others. In 59 percent of incidents, the shooter told more than one person.

The shooter previously used weapons

Exactly two-thirds, 63 percent, of students included in the Secret Service/Department of Education study had a known history of weapons use, including knives, guns and bombs. Over half, 59 percent, had experience with a gun prior to the incident. Less than half, 44 percent, demonstrated a fascination with weapons prior to the incident.

In some school systems, elementary students carry weapons as often and in some cases more often than middle and high school students. This is most likely because more measures are usually in place at secondary schools to prevent students from bringing weapons to school.

There is no uniform profile

Both the FBI study and the Secret Service/Department of Education study found that there was no uniform profile of a student who might turn violent. Knowing that an individual shares characteristics or traits with prior school shooters does little to advance the appraisal of risk. For example, see the following divergence in key areas:

♦ **Ethnic background** – Shooters came from a broad range of ethnic groups, although 85 percent were white males
♦ **Academic background** – Shooters varied from those receiving As and Bs, 41 percent; Bs and Cs, 15 percent; and Cs and Ds, 22 percent. Very few were failing, only 5 percent. For instance the shooter in Moses Lake, Washington was a 'straight A' student. In Paducah, Kentucky, the shooter was the brother of the school's valedictorian.

◆ **Social backgrounds** – Shooters varied from having no
   behavioral issues to having multiple relationship
   problems and suicidal tendencies.

The Secret Service/Department of Education report found
that, "a fact-based approach may be more productive in
preventing school shooting than a trait-based approach." An
example of using a fact-based approach regarding a specific
student would be noting if there was a communicated threat
to shoot another student or staff member, found weapon
and/or plans, or a tip from another student of specific
school shooting plans. A trait-based approach would be
based on only behavioral problems without any concrete
evidence.

If a teacher believes a potential risk exists, first consider if
there are concerning incidents, such as student tips or the
triggering behaviors of re-occurring fights, (fact-based). If
that is the case, then consider how student backgrounds, such
as personality and family life (trait-based) apply to the
situation in order to decide whether or not an intervention is
necessary and time critical.

Bystanders resolved the incident before authorities arrived

In 47 percent of incidents, the attackers were apprehended,
surrendered or stopped shooting within 15 minutes. School
officials or fellow students stopped the attacker before law
enforcement officers arrived in 27 percent of incidents, the

same percentage of incidents that were ended by law enforcement intervention.

Other students were involved

Although most incidents involved the attacker working alone, in 81 percent of incidents, at least one other person knew that the shooter was planning an attack before it occurred. In one case the attacker had arranged for another student to photograph the event. In the same incident, a student who rose late on the morning of the scheduled day of the shooting took a cab to school so they would not miss the shooting. In 44 percent of cases, the attacker was encouraged or dared by other individuals to carry out an attack.

Source: Vossekuil, et al, "The Final Report and Findings of the Safe School Initiative: Implications for the Prevention of School Attacks in the United States," United States Secret Service and United States Department of Education, Washington, D.C., May 2002.

Federal Bureau of Investigation, "The School Shooter: A Threat Assessment Perspective," 2000.

3.4 Behaviors that can lead to violence

Violent students almost always exhibit some form of communicative or unusual behavior before an outburst. In 93 percent of the incidents included in the Secret Service/Department of Education study, school officials, parents, teachers, police, and fellow students were concerned about the attackers behavior prior to an incident. In 88 percent of incidents, there was at least one adult who was concerned about the attacker's behavior. In one case, this has taken the form of poetry and essay writings that the teacher has described as "dark writings." In another case, the attackers created a simulated videotape of the proposed violence for a class project. Perhaps most significant was that 78 percent of the attackers, prior to the incident, either had made suicide attempts or exhibited a history of suicidal thoughts before the attack. By focusing on continual and attentive supervision of children, individual teachers can have a significant positive impact on the level of violence in a school.

3.4.1 "Red flags"

Each of the following lists of "red flags" can be helpful in understanding and responding to potential threats of student violence. There is no foolproof way for teachers to identify the next perpetrator of school violence; however, individuals that express these characteristics, and their families, need to be given special attention and support because they are potential signs of deeper dysfunction in the home.

The U.S. Department of Education has developed the following warning signs for students who may become violent:

Behavioral problems
- ◆   Social withdrawal
- ◆   Acute feelings of isolation

Having a strong network of friends can help lessen feelings of isolation and rejection **2003**/0562500

◆ Acute feelings of rejection
◆ Feelings of being picked on and persecuted
◆ Intolerance for differences
◆ Being a victim of violence
◆ Low school interest and poor academic performance
◆ Drug and alcohol use

Signs of violence (verbal or physical)
◆ Expression of violence in writings and drawings
◆ Uncontrolled anger
◆ Past history of violent aggressive behavior
◆ Patterns of impulsive hitting, intimidating and bullying behavior

- History of discipline problems
- Inappropriate access to guns
- Serious threats of violence
- Affiliation with gangs

Source: U.S. Department of Education, Early Warning, Timely Response, Washington, DC, 1998.

The National School Safety Center has developed the following summary of potential warning signs of students that may turn violent:

Behavioral problems
- On the fringe of their peer group with few or no close friends
- Preoccupation with weapons, explosives or other incendiary devices
- Previous truancy, suspensions or expulsions from school History of tantrums and uncontrollable angry outbursts
- Background of serious disciplinary problems at school and in the community
- Background of drug, alcohol or other substance abuse or dependency
- Habit of blaming others for difficulties and problems they cause themselves
- Often depressed and/or has significant mood swings
- Threatened or attempted suicide

Experienced victimization

◆ Has little or no supervision and support from parents or a caring adult

◆ Has witnessed or been a victim of abuse or neglect in the home

Signs of violence (verbal or physical)

◆ Name calls, curses or uses abusive language

◆ Makes violent threats when angry

◆ Brings weapons to school

◆ Bullies and/or intimidates peers or younger children

◆ Is a member of a gang or an antisocial group on the fringe of peer acceptance

◆ Displays cruelty to animals

◆ Prefers television shows, movies, music [or computer games] expressing violent themes and acts

◆ Prefers reading materials dealing with violent themes, rituals and abuse

◆ Reflects anger, frustration and the dark side of life in school essays or writing projects

Source: National School Safety Center, 1998, "Checklist of Common Traits of Violent Youth," School Safety Newsjournal, Fall 1998, http://www.nssc1.org/reporter/checklist.htm

3.4.2 Bullying

Bullying is a major factor in school violence. According to the Secret Service/Department of Education, 71 percent of attackers felt bullied or persecuted by others prior to the

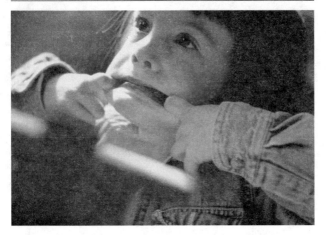

Any form of teasing or bullying should be discouraged
2004/0564600

incident. Many attackers, however, have engaged in bullying behavior before more serious incidents of violence. When left unchecked, bullying has clearly escalated to more serious forms of violence. Bullying behavior is more prevalent when students are not properly supervised. Negligent privacy may occur in a classroom or playground despite the presence of a teacher or other staff member.

In many incidents the attacker had demonstrated or talked to others about problems with bullying and feelings of isolation, anger, depression and frustration. These characteristics should alert school administrators, teachers and support staff to address the needs of troubled students through meetings with parents, the provision of school counseling, guidance and mentoring services, as well as referrals to appropriate community health/social services and law enforcement personnel. Such behavior should provide an early warning signal that safe school plans and emergency operations plans procedures must be in place to protect the health and safety of all school students and staff members. Schools should enforce appropriate behavior on the school campus and provide training programs that **focus on bullying prevention** and non-violent conflict resolution.

Source: Weakfish-Bullying Through the Eyes of a Child 2003 by Michael Dorn

Invisible kids

A teacher in an inner city school befriended a student who had recently transferred in from another inner city school across town. At first he was extremely withdrawn and almost hostile. But, as time passed, he confided that he had been bullied at his last school and the students there often made comments that he could be someone who would come to school with a gun. He fit perfectly the list of characteristics of the invisible kid.

The teacher would never have thought this student could be violent. The student found it funny that the students saw him this way. He was extremely insecure and really wanted to be accepted.

Invisible kids

These types of students can be victims, perpetrators or enablers of violence. The characteristics of invisible kids include:

♦ Above average in IQ
♦ Unmotivated
♦ Disenfranchised
♦ Have no appropriate adult role models
♦ Rarely present behavior problems
♦ Tend to be bullied rather than be the bully
♦ Very playful

Because the students exhibiting this behavior are associated with school violence, teachers can be proactive and can have a real impact on safety in the classroom.

Source: Shubert, T. H., Bressett, S. Deeken, J., & Bender, W. N., "Analysis of random school shootings," in Bender, W., Clinton, G., & Bender, R. Eds Violence Prevention and Reduction In Schools., Austin, TX.: ProEd, 1999.

3.5 Incidents preceding major acts of violence

Just as the behavioral issues of red flags, bullying and the "invisible kid" condition can lead to acts of larger-scale violence, smaller incidents, such as weapons possession and fights, can build into a crescendo of violence. This is more likely when the community of teachers, administrators, psychologists, counselors, security guards, school resource officers, parents and students do not to work together to prevent or resolve incidents quickly and/or do not follow through on set procedures.

3.5.1 Triggering behaviors

A review of hundreds of traditional weapons assaults in schools around the nation contained in *School/Law Enforcement Partnerships: A Guide to Police Work in Schools* revealed that most weapons assaults on and near campus involve identifiable violent acts known as "triggering behaviors." **The reduction of the frequency and severity of triggering behaviors is just as important as the reduction of weapons on campus, if not more so.**

While there are examples of individuals suffering from mental illness who have carried out attacks, most school weapons assaults involve the availability of a weapon and one or more triggering behaviors. For a weapon assault to occur, the following two factors must be present:

1. The presence of a weapon on campus. The weapon may be an item such as a firearm, knife or metal knuckles, or it may be an improvised weapon such as a pencil.
2. The desire on the part of an individual to use a weapon to harm another person.

Although school shootings are rarely impulsive, it is important to remember that many more typical incidents of weapon violence involve impulsive acts preceded by triggering behaviors. For example, one of the most common scenarios for a school weapons assault is a student using a weapon during a fistfight, most commonly a small knife or box cutter.

Examples of triggering behaviors

The following are the most commonly observed triggering behaviors that precede weapons violence in schools:

◆ Fights
◆ Intense verbal altercations
◆ Bullying
◆ Disrespectful gang behavior
◆ Extortion of lunch money

While the prevalence of each of these triggering behaviors and conditions will vary among schools and regions, a consistent pattern of associated weapons violence exists.

Source: School/Law Enforcement Partnerships: A Guide to Police Work in Schools by Mike Dorn 2002.

3.5.2 Fights and "negligent privacy"

Teachers can prevent violent behavior through the appropriate supervision of students. Teachers may need to reduce the incidence of "negligent privacy" that can involve giving students (or others) more privacy than they need and/or overlooking students' troubling words and body language. Fights typically do not erupt suddenly. Since observable behaviors, such as a verbal arguments or threatening gestures, precede fights in schools, not observing these behaviors can open the door to future violence. Teachers can better serve school safety through early and prompt intervention to prevent escalation by interrupting a violent situation before it has started. By focusing on continual and attentive supervision of children, individual teachers can have a significant positive impact on the level of violence in a school.

3.6 Teacher action points to prevent violence

Teachers who are aware of trends in student violence, pre-incident behavioral issues as well as the propensity for lower-level violence to escalate can use this knowledge to prevent school violence. Such teacher experience can also help the school and/or district design school safety programs using non-violent conflict resolution strategies. This ability requires a regular awareness of the school environment in terms of knowledge of past experiences as well as using broad-based procedures to prevent and respond to incidents of concern.

3.6.1 Teacher awareness

Teachers should be aware of common warning signs – based on research, social knowledge of the students, and past experience – and other unique instances that have surfaced at or near the school that could indicate violence. The following are general factors for teachers to pay attention to:

◆ Progression of students' low-level behaviors that turn into violence
◆ Time when a student exhibited a warning sign that lead to a violent incident
◆ Common location(s) where incidents take place
◆ Relationship between and/or reason for disputes and other conflict: gangs, drugs, interpersonal problems, romantic disputes

In the event there is a particular cause for concern, teachers must be proactive and follow through on deescalating any problems. In doing so, early intervention might stop more serious violent acts.

See *Chapter 6: How can teachers encourage students to help with school safety?* for guidance on building trust with students to learn about their view of the school's safety environment and the context of potential warning signs.

3.6.2 Teacher action points

It is possible for teachers to take swift action to resolve violent incidents as well as show students that harmful behavior is unacceptable. The following areas are action points teachers can use to decrease the incidence of violence in school.

♦ Learn about the student safety climate
♦ Talk and listen to students
♦ Promote student inclusiveness
♦ Enforce safety policies
♦ Respond to incidents

Learn about the student safety climate

♦ **Be aware of "dark writings,"** suicide attempts and other indications of an unsettled student
♦ **Combine a fact-based and trait-based approach;** look for concrete evidence of what the student is doing and saying that could indicate a propensity to violence. Then consider behavioral problems that will be present in select students across all types of schools.
♦ Expand attention on the social behavior and known background of all students, not only the "problem" students

Talk and listen to students

Having a solid rapport with all students is crucial to being an effective teacher and ensuring safety. Teachers can take the following measures:

♦ Talk to students about the need to report threats, students with weapons and events that can lead to violence, such as bullying
♦ Keep **communication open** with students
   • Welcome students to talk about problems in their

lives before they get out of hand, especially if these problems involve abuse at home or at school. Convince students that teachers are advocates for their needs and will unconditionally accept them.

◆ Always take student tips and comments seriously and report them to the appropriate school official
  ● Follow-up on the report to ensure action is taking place

Promote student inclusiveness

◆ Be alert for students who do not appear to fit in, especially if they resist group work
◆ **Do not allow students to tease, touch, or torment students.** An off-handed remark or teasing comment may seem harmless to adults but could be devastating to the student.
◆ Try to end the isolation of "invisible kids," self-imposed or otherwise
  ● Introduce the student to other nice students
  ● Approach students that are trustworthy and kind and ask them to befriend this student
  ● Approach the student outside of the classroom to discuss any subject that seems appropriate

Enforce safety policies

◆ Assist in enforcing school policies **prohibiting weapons** on campus clearly and consistently. Policies should clearly define what is and is not a weapon and spell out the consequences of a weapon violation. Elementary school students should be included in these efforts.

◆ Enforce consistently school policies designed to **reduce triggering behaviors**. The reduction of the frequency and severity of triggering behaviors, such as fights or bullying, is just as important as the reduction of weapons on campus, if not more so. Simply put, **every fistfight increases the chances that a shooting or stabbing will take place.**

Respond to incidents

◆ **Be prepared** to act as a **"first-responder"** to incidents of school violence. See *Chapter 4: Emergency response procedures: what do teachers do?* for guidance on response procedures

◆ **Do not ignore** a potentially violent situation or believe the situation will work itself out

◆ **Pay attention to verbal and non-verbal cues** that could lead to violence

  ● **Rumors or whispers of potential confrontations**
    – Gang activity
    – Drug deals
    – Personal animosity resulting from relationships
    – Weekend sport or social events

  ● **Noticeable gatherings of students.** These can signal fights because they are often scheduled so that there is an audience.

  ● **Student tips.** Take information or tips on any of these areas seriously and report to the

administration because often one of the participants
or friends of the participants will confide in a
teacher about the fight.

◆ **Report**: worrisome incidents to administrators, school
mental health staff, school resource officers, and the
student's parents

*NOTE: This guide does not recommend that teachers take
matters into their own hands to resolve violence, although it
does recognize that teachers will often resolve violent
incidents before the arrival of professional first responders to
the scene.*

3.6.3 Reporting procedures

Teachers should report concerns about potentially violent
students immediately to the appropriate school official. A
delay of even a few minutes could prove disastrous in some
situations. This is also true for information received after
school hours. In some cases, school staff have averted violent
situations because they promptly passed on information
received after hours.

A multidisciplinary team, established by the school to assess
threats and consisting of an administrator, school resource
officer, guidance counselor, a teacher and other appropriate
school staff, should develop a concrete process that allows
teachers and students to report concerns, receive a swift
response and protects their confidentiality. The school should
also provide teachers with a proper, thorough and careful

multidisciplinary assessment to gauge most situations accurately. This process seeks to protect innocent students and staff from potential danger. The following are general reporting guidelines:

◆ **Response** – report information accurately and promptly
◆ **Reason** – report any situations that cause concern. It is better to report a situation that may turn out to be harmless than allow a terrible event to occur.
  ● **Student threats** – take students' comments seriously and respond quickly if they talk about violent actions. Be sure to report any threats, verbal or written, to the appropriate administrator.
  ● **Known incidents** – report any suspicious phone calls, bomb threats, damage, theft or vandalism to school property. Do not be embarrassed to do so because this could alert the school to a possible greater risk.
  ● **Student tips** – listen actively when receiving information about a possible threat. Pay attention to details and ask questions as appropriate. It is not the teacher's role to conduct a threat assessment, but obtain enough information to forward to the appropriate point of contact.
◆ **Context** – Do not pre-judge students. Consider all of the available information: the student(s) involved, their relationship, known dangers (weapons, communicated threats, fights), related past incidents and the school safety climate.

◆ **Confidentiality**– respect student confidentiality when appropriate and possible

---

Student tips and administrator action

In 2003, a Pennsylvania elementary student concealed more than a half dozen rifles, shotguns and handguns in his waistband and entered his school intent on carrying out a planned school shooting. A student, who had previously heard him make threats, noticed that he entered a school bathroom wearing camouflage clothing and reported the situation to the Principal. The Principal ordered a lockdown and summoned police, likely preventing a large school shooting. The student unfortunately committed suicide in a school bathroom.

Following-up on teacher reports

After reporting observations and/or student tips about a possible violent situation to the administration, make sure the Principal, counselor, psychologist, security officer or the school resource officer (SRO) is handling the situation. Teachers should not be expected to handle this information or coordinate a response by themselves, but must make it clear that they are stakeholders in this process.

The FBI has developed a threat assessment model that administrators can use to respond to staff and student reports of violent incidents or associated risks, particularly with school shootings. Upon receiving reports, the administration should have a process to identify, assess and manage violent incidents or potentially harmful students and/or visitors.

Based on the FBI model, teachers should expect administrators to consider the following **fact-based** questions in a **timely** fashion upon receiving reports:

◆ How vague, specific or detailed is the risk?
◆ Is there motive?
◆ Does the student have the resources to carry out a violent act?
◆ Is there information on the time and place the incident (fight/attack/theft) is planned to occur?

Considering behavioral issues, administrators should then gather **trait-based** information on the personality, family, social and school dynamics of the individual(s) in question, known as the "four-pronged assessment." Following this assessment, administrators should act swiftly on the threat if it is deemed appropriate, in coordination with the appropriate law enforcement officials. Although the teacher's role is important, they may be peripheral to the process.

Source: Federal Bureau of Investigation, "The School Shooter: A Threat Assessment Perspective," 2000.

<u>NOTES</u>

Chapter 4

Emergency response procedures
– what do teachers do?

4.1 Introduction

Emergency situations stemming from conventional as well as unconventional sources can affect schools. It is important for teachers to have a clear understanding of how best to respond to and plan for emergencies. By knowing how to detect a broad range of potentially harmful incidents and how to initiate a response under tense situations, teachers can mitigate the effects of such threats and help return the class-room to a learning environment as quickly as possible.

Chapter overview

This chapter provides guidance on what teachers can do in the event of the following situations:

- Role during an incident
- Communications during an incident
- General emergency response procedures
- Specific emergency response procedures
- Medical emergencies
- Natural disasters
- Fire
- Child abuse
- Domestic violence
- Armed attackers and hostage situation
- Hazardous materials
- Man-made accidents/disasters
- Bomb threats
- Bomb/explosive devices

- Chemical/biological incidents
- Radiological/nuclear incidents

4.2 Role during an incident

Each person in the school community has a role to play during a crisis. The teacher's role is very important because he/she is in charge of keeping the students safe. Teachers are the first and last bulwarks against harm to students in many situations. Therefore, it is important for teachers to be well versed in the procedures the school and the district have in place and their role in carrying out those procedures.

The information in this section is meant to give general guidelines for teachers to prepare themselves to respond effectively in a crisis in tandem with training offered by the school district. It is equally important to note that the school's emergency operations plan should dictate responses to any emergency situation. The steps mentioned in this section are only examples of action steps that are commonly found in an emergency operations plan and are not meant to supersede response procedures provided by the school.

4.2.1 Pre-incident preparation

Responding to a crisis should begin long before a situation arises. Teachers can limit the effects of an incident by preparing in advance. Teachers are recommended to do the following before an incident occurs:

- Spend time studying the school's emergency operations plan. Be able to perform key functions and action steps by memory.
- Visualize how to perform emergency procedures in the context of the school's physical design and classroom layout
- Ensure that emergency operations plan components are readily available. Keep associated plan components nearby, such as flip charts or emergency cards.
- Keep emergency operation plans and components secure
- Maintain emergency supplies and response kits in good order
- Participate in training, drills or exercises. This is one of the best ways to prepare for a crisis situation.

4.2.2 Responding during an incident

Teachers are usually the first members of the school staff to face a crisis situation. Proper response procedures can save the lives of students and teachers, considering most damage occurs within the first 15 minutes of a crisis. Teachers are recommended to follow the general guidelines below in the event of an emergency:

- **Always follow the established response procedures the school has in place** as closely as possible under stressful situations
- Remain calm. A teacher's composure will have a major impact on the level of calmness of students.
- Assess the situation clearly and quickly

- Keep control over students at all times
- Act immediately according to the situation. Teachers may have to carry out initial actions before consulting emergency operations plan components or without direction from school administrators or emergency operations personnel.
- Refer to plan components as soon as possible. Locate the proper section(s) in the ready reference flip chart and quickly check listed action points against the actions already taken.
- Remain flexible. Required responses to an incident may change as the situation evolves.
- Take measures for self-protection. This benefits the teachers and the students. Teachers cannot protect students if they are incapacitated.
- Communicate with school administrators and emergency response officials as quickly and accurately as possible
- If evacuation is necessary, teachers should remember to bring the classroom emergency response kit, emergency plan components and attendance book

Teachers can limit the effects of an incident by maintaining emergency supplies and response kits

2004/0564605/0564604/0564603

♦   Control the use of portable phones as appropriate.
    Portable phones can create great difficulties and dangers
    for teachers and emergency responders. If the school's
    policy allows, students should not be allowed to call the
    media, parents, or others.

4.3 Communications during an incident

The chaos of a school crisis or disaster can affect the abilities
of many involved to respond. Initial confusion and panic can
make it difficult for those directly impacted by a crisis to
clearly communicate with those who provide support.
Knowing the procedures and tools for effective
communication, however, can facilitate the resolution of a
crisis.

If there is an emergency, teachers must be able to communicate important information to the school administration
and emergency responders. This section will discuss how
teachers can communicate information effectively and
tools teachers may have at their disposal to convey a need for
help.

4.3.1 Reporting an incident

A teacher's call for help can possibly save lives, minimize
damage or help to locate perpetrators. Teachers should report
an incident as soon and as accurately as possible while
remaining calm. When teachers call for help, they should try
to avoid speaking too fast and should use a clear tone. In all

cases, they should watch and report any emergency from a safe location. Teachers should also provide their names and contact information to public safety officials for follow-up questions. When calling from a cell phone, they should give the dispatcher their cell phone number and keep the phone on in case further information is needed.

Teachers can assist the efforts of emergency responders by explaining key information. The CHALET method below is a useful guide for determining what information emergency responders may need to know. Teachers should always provide their contact information for follow-up questions.

Casualties resulting from the incident
◆ Number of casualties observed
◆ Kind of injuries suffered
◆ Location
◆ Odors and/or sounds

Hazards in the incident area
◆ Fires
◆ Ruptured gas or water mains
◆ Exposed electrical cables
◆ Visible plumes of unknown substances
◆ Buildings or structures that appear unstable

Access routes available to travel to and evacuate the scene
◆ Access routes – roads, highways, piers, bridges – available for travel and evacuation

- Quality of routes, if any obstruction exits along them such as fallen tree, parked cars

Location of resources
- Where helicopters could land to evacuate critical casualties (Ideally sites clear of debris with no overhanging cover, such as trees, power lines, sand and/or large rock formations, etc.)
- Location of fire hydrants

Emergency personnel already on the scene
- Services may be needed that are not currently present
- State of response efforts on the scene (Are responders overwhelmed? Do they appear to have the situation under control?)

Type of incident or indicators of an emergency
- School violence
- Natural disaster
- Human-caused disaster/accident
- Fire

Source: The section above was adapted from the reporting section of *Jane's Citizen's Safety Guide*.

4.3.2 Tools for communicating to administrators and first responders

Sending for help can be done in many ways, but teachers and administrators should keep in mind several special considerations. Redundancy in emergency communications is important. This entails the ability to use multiple forms of communication in the event that primary communications systems become damaged or overloaded. Cellular, digital and traditional telephone systems can often become unreliable and clogged with traffic when a major school crisis occurs. Teachers and administrators should also consider that sending students to relay messages about an incident or crisis can in some instances endanger their well-being. Classroom phones, portable radios and cellular phones are some of the tools teachers may have at their disposal, depending upon the school district.

Classroom phones

For schools without an intercom system or whose only means of communication is in person, having a phone in the classroom is one solution. Teachers have used classroom phones for anything from contacting the main office to let them know they are sending a sick child to the nurses office or to report a suspicious person in the building. Other day-to-day uses include calling parents if a child has been absent for several days. Distinct disadvantages exist, however, for example when a phone rings and disrupts class. As with cell phone systems, conventional telephone systems can also become damaged or overloaded during an emergency, rendering them inoperable. Classroom phones are not portable and cannot be used if the class is evacuating.

Portable radios

Portable radios, in some schools, are a primary emergency communications tool for teachers and school officials. In most situations, they are one of the most fast and reliable means of emergency communication. They do have disadvantages, such as:

◆ Communications are easily intercepted by media or a person carrying out a violent attack

◆ If a perpetrator takes a radio, s/he can both eavesdrop on responders and interfere with communications by keying the microphone. Since only one person can transmit on a channel at one time, doing so blocks the use of all other radios operating on that channel.

◆ Excited staff members can block others by talking for long periods of time

◆ Portable radios can become hazards during bomb threats by creating radio frequency energy that could detonate some bomb types

◆ Teachers will not be able to talk to first responders unless a function for various groups to communicate with one another on a common channel is enabled

Cellular phones

Cellular and digital telephones offer many of the same advantages and are subject to many of the same limitations as portable radios. They are also more subject to failure due to heavy call volume during a major school crisis. Normally, once a line has been established by cell phone to a remote location, such as with emergency responders, teachers should keep the connection open for as long as possible. It may be impossible to get another connection later. Not all teachers will have access to cell phones because of their cost. Some school districts do distribute cell phones to all teachers, but in most cases, teachers may use personal cell phones.

Notification (call-down) lists

Call-down lists are used mainly by the head administrator or principal. They are lists containing the names, phone and pager numbers of pre-arranged crisis response team (CRT) members and other key personnel during emergencies. In some cases, the call-down process is carried out at a facility that is not on the same phone system as the affected school or central school system. This practice enables the call-down process to continue when the main school and school system phone numbers are clogged due to high call volume. They have been considered valuable tools when critical information needed to be disseminated rapidly. Teachers should be aware of the call-down list procedures in the event they are asked to assist in the notification process.

4.3.3 Signal cards

Teachers can display signal cards in a classroom window or hold them up during evacuation to let emergency response personnel know the status of their students. They are useful because they allow CRT members and public safety officials to spot problems from a distance. One example set includes green, yellow, red and white with a large red cross cards (corresponding to codes established by the school district). As with other emergency codes and procedures, these cards should be standardized throughout the school system.

Source: Adapted from *Jane's Safe Schools Planning Guide for All Hazards*, and *Jane's School Safety Handbook, Second Edition.*

4.3.4 Ready reference flip chart

A ready reference flip chart consists of clear, easy-to-use, step-by-step instructions for all the emergency situations a school is likely to face. Charts are usually consistent with the district's emergency operations plan and individual emergency response plans. In many school districts, teachers are issued flip charts for their use during actual emergencies. The contents of the flip chart will usually differ between school districts as well as between schools within the same district.

4.4 General emergency response procedures

General emergency response procedures (called functional protocols by the emergency management community) are written action steps implemented during an emergency or crisis situation. Evacuation, shelter-in-place, lock-down, parent/student reunification and reverse evacuation are just some examples of these general procedures. These response procedures can be used in many different types of situations and often act as component actions to be followed within incident-specific protocols.

Incident-specific protocols explain how to respond to particular situations like a bomb threat or hazardous material (HazMat) spill. Teachers should be familiar with procedures whether general or specific because they are an integral part of the response to all types of disasters.

4.4.1 Evacuation

Evacuation is a process by which staff and students leave the school building in a calm and orderly fashion to a pre-determined site. Evacuation procedures should be completed only upon the advice of school administrators or emergency management personnel. Teachers should take the following actions to carry out an evacuation protocol:

- Organize students to act in a calm and orderly fashion
- Lead students to pre-arranged evacuation site or secondary site if necessary
- **Do not take shortcuts** as they may lead to danger
- Bring emergency response kit
- Make sure there are provisions for special needs students, especially mobility-impaired students

4.4.2 Shelter-in-place

When the dangers of evacuating the school outweigh those of taking cover in a school building, school administrators or emergency responders will order teachers to "shelter-in-place." This can be done, for example, during natural disasters and health hazards. Although sheltering-in-place will take different forms for different emergencies, teachers should take the following measures when asked to perform this general response procedure:

♦ Take shelter in an appropriate area (i.e. – in a basement or an inside room for a tornado, or a sealable room for a chemical or biological attack) if directed to do so by proper authorities
♦ Close doors and windows
♦ Stay away from windows and move to center of room
♦ Seal air vents and gaps under doors and around windows with duct tape and plastic sheeting (if trying to keep out chemical/biological/radiological contaminants)
♦ Monitor local radio and television for the latest emergency information and instructions. Remain in shelter until the authorities indicate that it is safe to come out
♦ Shut down ventilation (if necessary)
♦ Stay sheltered until otherwise notified by appropriate officials

4.4.3 Lockdown

Lockdowns are used to keep dangerous people from gaining access to children and staff in the school. Administrators may also order a lockdown if local authorities are searching the premises for a specific student, group, teacher or item, such as with a drug bust. Teachers need to be trained on how to calm their students and have the resources to help when their students need physical or psychological help. Teachers should take the following measures when asked to perform this function:

- Immediately lock doors and pull blinds to classroom
- Turn off classroom light
- Use signaling methods provided by school (e.g. color coded cards) to let administrators and emergency responders know the condition of people in room
- Do not provide access to room for people other than administrators or emergency management personnel. It may be necessary to verify credentials before providing access to strangers.

4.4.4 Parent/student reunification

Teachers should be prepared for the aftermath of a major event and the often difficult process of releasing students back to their parents. To ensure that the reunification process goes as smoothly as possible, teachers may need to do the following:

- Carry release forms, signed by parents/guardians, for each student with the names of persons to be notified if a parent/guardian cannot be contacted; at least two people other than the parents should have permission to take students home if a parent is unavailable
- Access student release information to determine which students were released prior to the crisis

4.5 Response procedures for specific incidents

The following sections will provide recommended response procedures for teachers to follow during specific types of emergencies. The emergency management community calls these incident-specific protocols. In keeping with the all hazards approach to school safety, this guide includes examples of response procedures for most of the threats a school is likely to face.

The response procedures listed in this book can serve as sample checklists for teachers to use in their classroom. Many school districts issue a standard checklist to make sure a class is ready to respond in an emergency situation. It is advised that teachers keep these checklists in a central location to remind themselves and students of important safety measures throughout the day. **Teachers who create their own checklists should confirm that they follow the school's emergency operations plans.**

4.6 Medical emergencies

Recognizing life-threatening medical conditions and acting appropriately and quickly after an injury or the onset of a serious illness is crucial. Teachers are most familiar with the medical conditions of students and are likely to be the first to deal with injuries to students. Often, teachers will be the first to deal with a sick or injured student before the school health or emergency responders can arrive. Teachers should only provide care as the situation or their training dictates. They should contact the school nurse immediately in case of a medical emergency. If a teacher believes someone could suffer significant harm or die unless they receive immediate

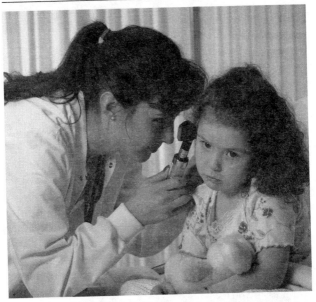

Teachers should call the school nurse or emergency services to treat serious illness or injury   **2004**/0564601

attention, they should immediately **call the emergency services.** Teachers should watch out for warning signs of a serious illness or injury, including:

◆ Uncontrolled bleeding
◆ Sudden or acute pain
◆ Chest pain lasting several minutes
◆ Coughing/vomiting blood

- Shortness of breath, breathing problems
- Weakness, dizziness or change in vision
- Altered or unusual mental state (drowsiness, confusion and so on)
- Severe or persistent vomiting or diarrhea

If someone is exhibiting one or more of these symptoms:

- Contact school nurse and principal
- **Immediately call the emergency services**
- **Do not move** anyone involved in a serious fall or found unconscious unless they are in immediate danger of further injury
- Do not give the victim anything to eat or drink
- **Protect the victim** by keeping them covered
- If the victim is bleeding, apply a clean cloth or sterile bandage. If possible, elevate the injury and apply direct pressure on the wound.
- If the victim is not breathing or does not have a pulse, begin rescue breathing or CPR (if trained)
- Avoid direct contact with blood or other body fluids
- Use protective equipment such as gloves
- Wash hands thoroughly with soap and water immediately after providing care

The following first aid techniques, however, can be used to provide assistance to someone who is hurt but whose injuries are not life threatening.

4.6.1 Basic first aid

Bleeding

Blood born pathogens are a major worry. Hepatitis, HIV and other diseases may be passed through bodily fluids. Special precautions should be taken anytime bodily fluids are involved.

- Be sure to put on personal protective equipment first including goggles and latex gloves
- Cover the wound and apply direct pressure
- Raise the injured area above the level of the heart (if broken bones are not suspected)
- Cover the wound with a roller bandage
- If the bleeding does not stop apply additional dressings and use a pressure point to squeeze the artery against the bone

Burns
- Cool the burnt area with large amounts of water
- Cover with dry, clean dressings or cloth

Muscles, bones or joints
- Rest the injured part
- Apply ice or a cold pack to control any swelling and reduce pain
- Avoid any movement that causes pain
- If the victim must be moved (if the location is unsafe), attempt to immobilize the injured part

Shock

Shock is a common reaction to injury regardless of the severity and is most likely to appear in the first hour after an injury. If left untreated, **shock can be fatal** through the sudden decrease in blood pressure and therefore flow of blood and oxygen to vital organs. The symptoms of shock include the following:

- Slow, shallow breathing
- Pale, cool, clammy skin
- Lightheadedness and fainting
- Weak, rapid or absent pulse
- Staring eyes; pupils may be dilated
- Individual may be confused and have difficulty thinking or speaking clearly
- Individual may be unconscious

First aid for shock victims should include the following measures:

- **Remain calm** and speak to the victim in a reassuring voice
- **Raise their legs** above the heart (if broken bones are not suspected). If the victim is vomiting or bleeding from the mouth lay them on their side.
- Keep the victim from becoming cold or overheated
- Check for injuries and provide first aid as appropriate
- Loosen clothing that may restrict blood flow
- Do not give the victim food or water

4.6.2 Food poisoning

Food poisoning can affect a student, teacher, or an entire class. Teachers should be aware of the following procedures to help deal with incidents of food poisoning:

♦ Notify school administration and emergency services
♦ Isolate affected students/employees for treatment
♦ Notify custodial staff regarding clean up
♦ Notify cafeteria manager regarding possible problem causes and not to discard food
♦ Notify teachers in private regarding symptoms and action to take
♦ Note all students who are ill
♦ Keep accurate record of incident
♦ If intentional, contact police

4.7 Natural disasters

When a natural disaster threatens a school, the administration will monitor local radio and television broadcasts and act on the advice of the emergency services. If enough **advance warning** is available, school may be canceled for the day. It is easier to keep teachers and students at home than to send them home during a hurricane, tornado or other disaster.

The following guidelines have been derived from information published by the Federal Emergency Management Agency (FEMA) on what to consider when responding to natural disasters.

4.7.1 Severe weather

All schools, especially those in locations prone to severe weather such as **winter storms, thunderstorms, extreme heat** or **floods,** should have procedures in place to assess the risk to students and teachers.

The decision on whether to **cancel school** will be made by school or district officials. The school should have procedures in place to inform students and teachers of the decision to cancel work (call lists, hot line for employees to call for information, prior agreements with media outlets, etc.).

4.7.2 Tornado

Teachers should be aware of tornado response plans, especially in areas vulnerable to tornadoes. An area within each facility should be designated as a **tornado shelter**. This should ideally be in the **basement**. If the facility does not have a basement, the shelter should be an **interior room** on the lowest floor (inner hallway, restroom, etc.) with few or no windows. In high-rise buildings, where there may be no time to go to the basement, use an area in the center of the building.

In areas where tornadoes are a rare but possible occurrence, schools should still have response procedures. Not being in a recognized tornado zone is not a good enough reason not to have a basic response plan.

What to look for

If a tornado watch (indicating that a tornado may occur) is issued, teachers should do the following:

◆   Be alert to changing weather conditions
◆   Danger signs include:
   ●   A cloud of **debris**
   ●   The **sound** of a tornado (the noise has been likened to that of a freight train)
   ●   Tornadoes usually take place near the **trailing edge of thunderstorms**

Response procedures

If a tornado warning is issued (indicating that a tornado has been sighted nearby), teachers should do the following:

◆   If inside, go directly to the **designated tornado shelter**
◆   **Direct students to get under a piece of strong furniture** and use arms to protect their heads and neck
◆   Avoid sheltering in areas with a large span roof
◆   If outside, go the basement of the nearest **sturdy building** or lie flat in a **ditch or low-lying area**

4.7.3 Hurricane

In areas subject to hurricanes, school officials will monitor local weather and news channels. If a hurricane watch is issued indicating that there is a threat of a hurricane within the next 24–36 hours, most **districts will cancel school.**

If a hurricane warning is issued (indicating that a hurricane is expected in less than 24 hours) and it is too late to leave the area, teachers should do the following:

Response procedures

♦ Monitor local weather and news channels (radio and television) for warnings and information, or receive this information from school office

♦ **Stay inside and away from windows**, glass doors and so on

♦ Keep a supply of flashlights, batteries, food and water

♦ Be aware that the worst part of the hurricane happens once the "eye" has passed over and the **winds blow from the opposite direction**

♦ **Be alert for tornadoes** which can take place during and after a hurricane

♦ Stay away from **flood waters**

4.7.4 Earthquake

Earthquakes can occur without warning any time of the day. Earthquake zones are usually well defined and schools usually know if they are at risk for experiencing an earthquake. Earthquakes do occur outside of normal areas, such as the 4.5 magnitude earthquake centered near Richmond, Virginia in December 2003. All schools should be aware of the simple procedures below for use in the event of an earthquake.

Response procedures

Depending on your location, there are several measures that should be taken during an earthquake.

- If teachers and students are indoors:
  - Instruct students to **drop, cover and hold**
  - **Take cover** in the previously identified safe place
  - **Stay inside. Do not leave the building** to avoid being hit by falling debris.
- If outdoors when an earthquake hits:
  - Move into an **open area** away from buildings, power lines and so on
  - **Stay in the open** until the shaking stops
- If driving a vehicle:
  - **Slow down**
  - **Drive to a clear area** away from buildings, power lines and so on
  - **Stay** in the vehicle until the shaking stops
- **Stay out of and away from damaged buildings**
- Once the earthquake has stopped **proceed with extreme caution**. Roads, bridges and buildings may have been damaged.
- Listen to radio and television for the latest emergency information and instructions

Although smaller than the main earthquake, **aftershocks** can continue for hours, days or weeks and can **cause additional damage**, particularly to already weakened structures.

4.8 Fire

Teachers are usually most familiar with preparations for fire emergencies. Teachers should follow exactly the established procedures of their schools. The following is general information to consider when responding to a fire.

♦ **Call the emergency services**
♦ **Evacuate students from the building** in an orderly manner and proceeding to the designated **evacuation area(s)**
♦ **Bring emergency response kit**
♦ **Keep students calm and organized at all times**
♦ **Account for all students** once at the designated evacuation area(s)

The following actions should be taken during a fire-related evacuation:

♦ **Remain calm**
♦ If there is smoke present, stay **low to the ground and cover your mouth**
♦ If clothes catch fire, **stop, drop to the ground and roll**
♦ If there is smoke or fire in the nearest escape route, use an alternate escape route. If exiting through smoke, crawl low under the smoke and cover mouth with a wet cloth.
♦ If escaping through a closed door, feel the door and the door handle/knob with the back of your hand before

opening it. If they are warm, use an alternative escape route.

♦   If smoke, heat or flames block exit routes, **stay in the room with the door closed and signal for help** using a bright-colored item at the window. If there is a telephone in the room, call the fire department and tell them their exact location (floor, room number and so on).

♦   **NEVER use elevators**

♦   **DO NOT** risk life by attempting to **extinguish the fire**

♦   **DO NOT** waste time by collecting **personal items or by going back for students or colleagues. Doing so can risk death or injury. It is best to leave the building and notify fire officials of the location of other victims, so that they can make the rescue.**

♦   **ALWAYS** follow fire department instructions

4.9 Child abuse

Child abuse can be a very sensitive subject for teachers to deal with. They may be the first to learn about abuse at home or at school. Teachers and administrators may become aware, by seeing physical bruising on a student or from complaints of students, about abuse in another student's home. This must be reported to police even though it did not occur on school grounds. Teachers must make the student feel safe by dealing with any child abuse allegation swiftly and anonymously. Teachers can also be accused of child abuse after behavior they consider innocent, like breaking up a physical scuffle. Teachers must be aware of their own

actions and others to avoid potential child abuse cases in the
school.

4.9.1 Physical abuse

Whenever a school employee or volunteer hits a student or
aggressively comes into physical contact with a student, a
potential for a child abuse case arises. Quick investigation by
the appropriate authorities will allow student witnesses to
give an accurate account of abuse, if any, before they forget
or embellish their memories of the alleged incident.

4.9.2 Sexual abuse

Sexual abuse usually occurs in situations where school
employees or volunteers work or interact with a student one-
on-one. This could be when acting as a club sponsor, coach,
counselor, tutor, etc. Teachers should be aware of how one-
on-one or off-campus meetings with students appear, even if
they are for legitimate reasons.

Allegations regarding sexual child abuse may develop from a
sexual harassment complaint, a rumor or a complaint of
inappropriate physical contact by an employee towards a
child. All rumors should be investigated for any basis by
school administrators. Again, when someone reports an
alleged sexual abuse case it must be reported to the police
immediately. Schools should have a harassment investigation
policy and plan to deal with allegations.

4.9.3 Response procedures

The following are general recommendations to help teachers deal with allegations of abuse by a student against a school employee:

♦   Keep the student in a private location
♦   Notify the Principal/Superintendent
♦   Notify the police
♦   Notify child services
♦   If sexual, make sure a sexual assault counselor is involved
♦   A child abuse case is confidential and should not be discussed with persons without the need to know

---

Irate parent enters classroom

Irate parents, relatives, boyfriends, girlfriends, etc. have been known to enter a building to confront a student or an employee. One such incident occurred when a parent entered the building without checking into the office. She found her daughter's classroom. As she entered she picked up an electrical cord and began beating her daughter. The teacher did not know what to do.

4.10 Domestic violence

Domestic arguments involving school employees and students can extend to school property. Law enforcement officers are experienced in handling domestic situations and should be called immediately during such incidents. Employees and parents should be encouraged to tell principals or supervisors

---

when they have restraining orders against an individual so that staff may be alert to any intrusions. An employee assistance plan, if available, can be a valuable resource for employees. The school counselors will follow up on domestic violence problems as well. In most states, there is a domestic violence or child abuse hot line. Teachers need to be familiar with these numbers and call if they suspect a problem.

4.10.1 Response procedures

Before an incident happens, schools should carefully restrict and document visitors to the school to prevent any violence, including domestic violence, from happening on school grounds. Teachers must make sure these procedures are followed and should try to keep in touch with worries that students may have about a situation like this happening.

- Call police
- Lockdown classroom if directed to do so
- Secure individuals threatened
- Give as much information as possible to responding officers

Source: Mickie Mathes, Teacher's Workshop,
http://www.teachersworkshop.com

4.11 Armed attackers and hostage situations

Schools are particularly sensitive about attacks from armed individuals or groups. No two attacks are the same. Factors ranging from the attacker's motive, their knowledge of the facility layout, their weapon(s), the location and type of facility and the number of employees, or visitors can all influence the course and outcome of an incident. An incident that begins as a "straightforward" armed robbery can turn quickly into an armed standoff with hostages.

After the September 11, 2001 terrorist attacks, many individuals will take the approach of those on United Airlines Flight 93 and intervene themselves. The decision on whether or not to intervene will be made by individuals, some of whom will decide to take action. **Teachers, however, should be advised not to resist an attacker and prevent students from doing the same.**

The following are therefore generic checklists for teachers to consider when dealing with an incident involving an armed attacker. If an armed attacker is not in the classroom, initiate lockdown procedures immediately and wait for law enforcement or school administration to announce otherwise. If the attacker enters the classroom, take the following response procedures.

4.11.1 Armed individual in the school

- ◆ **Remain calm** and try to avoid escalating the incident
- ◆ **Keep students calm and quiet.** Prevent students from condemning or belittling the attacker.
- ◆ **Comply with the demands** of the individual(s) as completely as possible
- ◆ **NEVER argue**
- ◆ **Do not make any sudden movements** that could startle the individual. Keep your hands visible.
- ◆ **Do not** come between the attacker and the exit
- ◆ Persuade the attacker to talk without pointing the weapon. Reassure the attacker, by using a calm voice.
- ◆ **Do not** try to approach the attacker
- ◆ **Remain control of students' actions; instruct them to be silent and follow the teacher's lead**
- ◆ **Do not** attempt to disarm or tackle the individual
- ◆ If possible, talk to the individual and try to find out what they want. **Do not make promises** that you are not in a position to keep.
- ◆ Provide **first aid** to student's who have been injured
- ◆ Assess **possible escape routes**
- ◆ Make a mental note of the individual's physical appearance and the characteristics of the weapon(s)

If the attacker indicates intent to harm by pointing a weapon or making a threat, remain calm. Obviously, this is very difficult to do, but panic can only exacerbate the situation. The teacher will most likely be able to encourage the attacker to remain calm. If possible, notify the security staff or school resource officer and the Principal's office immediately.

These few guidelines should not be mistaken for extensive training. They may allow the teacher, however, to reach some understanding with the attacker, and calm the situation during the initial danger period. It may be possible for the teacher to excuse the class, and remain with the attacker alone. By using non-threatening actions, and a calm voice, teachers may also be able to control the situation, and, in a best-case scenario, request that the attacker hand over the weapon.

4.11.2 Hostage situation

A nightmare situation for teachers is that students will be taken hostage. Teachers may be taken hostage along with their students. In this situation, the teacher's primary goal is to keep students calm and orderly so as not to exacerbate the situation. Teachers should try to protect themselves as much as possible so that they can in turn protect their students.

If an attacker actually directs a weapon at a student or teacher, this is considered a hostage situation. In this case, the following actions are appropriate:

♦   Move back from involved interaction with the attacker and let the police hostage negotiators manage the situation. They have extensive training whereas the teacher probably does not.

♦   A general rule of thumb from that point on is to speak to

the attacker only when asked a direct question
- Speak in a calm voice and offer reassurances
- The goal at this point should be to not "come between" the attacker and the hostage negotiator who, hopefully, will soon appear on the scene
- If the attacker is a student, the teacher's relationship with the student may get in the way of the hostage negotiator's development of a relationship

There are a number of things that teachers should not do in a hostage situation:

- **Do not** confront an attacker with a weapon or approach the attacker. Either of these actions can be seen as threats.
- Never approach an attacker with a gun and dare him/her to pull the trigger
- **Do not** promise the attacker a successful resolution to the problem. Teachers cannot effectively make these promises and the attacker may react negatively.

If teachers are not taken hostage, they should maintain a safe distance and perform the following steps:

- Notify police, and give them information on:
  - The number of hostages and their names
  - Location of attacker(s) and hostages within the facility and a map of the facility
  - Direct dial telephone number of the office/location

of the hostage within the facility
- Possible connections the hostage has with the armed individual (for instance student attackers)
◆ Notify principal
◆ Evacuate students to an off-site, predetermined location when police announce it is safe
◆ Obtain as much descriptive information as possible regarding people involved, location of incident, weapons involved, map of school, etc.
◆ Check rosters to make sure all students are accounted for during lockdown and at evacuation site
◆ Notify student services for counselors
◆ Release students to parents

Attacks and rescue attempts
◆ If gunfire breaks out, **find cover** immediately
◆ Explosions of **tear gas may announce** a rescue attempt by the police. The room will quickly fill with tear-gas and trained police officers.
◆ **Instruct all students to find cover** and remain still
◆ Remain still until a police officer gives contrary instructions; **do not stand up** simply because the situation appears controlled
◆ Listen for and obey the commands of trained police officers.
◆ Realize that the **police will probably handcuff everyone** in the room, at least until they establish what has happened

A teacher's best judgment is his/her best ally. Judgment, coupled with these guidelines, should assist any teacher in getting through these difficult situations. Most hostage situations, if they progress past the initial formation of the hostage situation, are resolved without violence. That knowledge can provide calm during an extremely stressful situation.

4.11.3 Armed robbery

◆ Robbers' **motivation is usually cash or valuables** – they **rarely want to hurt anyone** and seldom harm those who cooperate

◆ Tell the robber that you will do what they want

◆ Keep students calm and encourage them to comply with demands

◆ The longer the robbery takes the more nervous and dangerous the robber becomes

◆ **Remain calm and cooperate. Make sure students follow the teacher's lead.**

◆ Inform the robber if there are other employees in another office or room – **make sure there are no surprises**

◆ **Give them all the cash/valuables that they demand**

◆ **Do not attempt to tackle or chase the robber**. To do either is to **invite violence.**

◆ Use the silent alarm (in retail establishments) only if you can do so wholly unnoticed by the robber. Otherwise wait until the robber has left the premises before raising the alarm.

- Make a mental note of the individual's physical **appearance** and the **characteristics of the weapon(s)**
- **Preserve the crime scene**. Do not touch, move or disturb any possible evidence.

Some schools have **standard robber description forms** that should be completed as soon as possible after the incident. Teachers should write down as detailed a description of the robber as possible and record everything they said.

4.11.4 Self-inflicted violence
Self-inflicted violence is an extremely sensitive issue for teachers to deal with. Teachers may be the only person a student trusts and can avert a suicide attempt. The following are general guidelines for teachers on how to deal with self-inflicted violence.

Threat of suicide
- Take the suicide threat seriously
- Advise the Principal or crisis response team (CRT) leader as soon as possible regarding the child's dilemma
- Call the student's parents immediately or as school procedures indicate
- Remain with the child at all times until a parent/guardian arrives. If the parent does not come, call child services or the police.
- Do not state that the child is "over-reacting" and that "it's really not that bad" (The child might view killing him/herself as a solution. Things might, in fact, be "that

bad" in his/her eyes.)
- Ask the child if they have a plan or intend to hurt
  him/herself. Ask for the details, if the answer is "yes."
  (The more defined the plan, the more serious the child is
  about attempting suicide)
- Refer the child's name to the guidance counselor
- Follow-up on the suicide threat

Suicide attempt
- Call 911 immediately
- Advise the Principal immediately
- Refer the child's name to the guidance counselor
- Stop rumors immediately
- If a weapon is involved, call security or the school
  resource officer immediately. A teacher should never
  attempt to disarm a person with a weapon.

Suicide completion
Teachers should follow school procedures to determine how
and when to do the following if a student or staff member
commits suicide:

- Contact principal immediately
- Clear the immediate area
- Contact the district guidance and psychology
  departments for strategies to stabilize the school
  environment
- Teachers should be informed in person of the facts of the
  situation before, and separately from, their students, who

should then be informed in person by the Principal or teacher

◆ Advise staff to be observant for additional trauma or concerns from close friends

◆ Set up a conference room to allow students to receive immediate counseling upon demand to confront their emotions regarding the loss

4.12 Hazardous materials and human-caused disasters and accidents

Each school should have appropriate procedures in place for dealing with hazardous materials and human-caused disasters/accidents. Teachers should know of these procedures and follow them. The following is general information to consider when responding.

4.12.1 Hazardous materials

The risks posed by chemicals and other hazardous materials (HazMat) are not limited to manufacturing sites. HazMat incidents can happen at any time and place, from transport accidents in urban areas involving hazardous materials to a chemical spill inside a facility. The October-November 2003 closing of Ballou High School in Washington, DC for clean-up after an intentional mercury contamination demonstrates that schools are not immune to hazardous materials leaks, especially if they are deliberate.

The following guidelines regarding hazardous materials have been derived from information published by the Federal Emergency Management Agency (FEMA).

What to look for

♦ Many hazardous materials do not have a taste or odor. Teachers and students can be exposed to a hazardous material even though they cannot see or smell it.

♦ Some hazardous materials cause a physical reaction (watering eyes, nausea and so on)

♦ Some hazardous materials can be recognized by an oil or foam-like appearance

♦ In the event of a major hazardous materials accident the authorities will provide the following information:
  - Type of hazard
  - Area affected
  - Protection measures
  - Evacuation routes (if necessary)
  - Shelter locations
  - Medical facilities locations
  - Phone numbers for extra assistance

♦ Teachers should watch for symptoms of chemical poisoning, including:
  - Difficulty breathing
  - Changes to skin color
  - Headache, blurred vision or dizziness
  - Irritated eyes, skin and throat
  - Unusual behavior

- Clumsiness or lack of coordination
- Stomach cramps, diarrhea

Response procedures

◆ **Do not remain in an area** if a toxic substance is seen or smelled or if someone has been overcome by toxic fumes/substances. Evacuate with students if directed to do so.

◆ **NEVER walk into, touch** or try to dispose of any spilled substances

◆ **Do not breathe gases or fumes.** If possible, cover mouth and nose with a damp cloth while leaving the area.

◆ If outside, move students **uphill**, **upwind** and **upstream** of a hazardous materials accident scene

◆ **Shelter-in-place if instructed to do so by emergency services personnel**

◆ **Evacuate** students from the area if advised by the authorities
  - **Take attendance** of students after evacuation
  - Bring **emergency response kit**

◆ **Do not eat or drink food or water that** may have been contaminated

◆ **Do not** provide medical care to victims of a hazardous materials incident until the authorities have **identified the substance** and have indicated it is safe to go near victims
  - Move victims into **fresh air** and call **emergency medical services**

- **Remove contaminated clothing** and shoes and place them in a plastic bag
- Follow directions in *4.15.3 Personal decontamination procedures*
- Unless the authorities have instructed not to use water on the particular substance involved, pour **cold water over the skin and eyes** of those who have come into contact with the substance until professional assistance arrives. Flush eyes from the nose outwards.
- If water is not available **carefully brush the substance off the skin** and away from the victim. If the substance is on the face, neck or shoulders ensure the victim shuts their eyes before removing the substance.
- Cover the affected area with a dry, sterile (or clean) cloth. The cloth should not stick to the wound.
- Do not put any medication on the affected area.

4.12.2 Human-caused disasters/accidents

Gas leak

- If gas is smelled in or around the facility, **evacuate students immediately** (although natural gas is odorless, providers add a distinctive-smelling chemical to enable detection)
- Take attendance of students
- Notify fire department
- Notify maintenance

- Notify the Principal/Superintendent
- **Do not** use electric switches, including telephones, cell phones and pagers, or anything that could **cause a spark**
- Extinguish all open flames (such as cigarettes)
- **Ventilate** the building by opening windows and doors
- Restrict access to the affected area

Elevator entrapment

There are a number of important safety measures that should be taken in the event of entrapment.

- Use the emergency contact phone or alarm to call for help
- **Remain calm** and **do not panic**
- **NEVER attempt to pry open the doors**
- **NEVER attempt to leave the elevator,** for example, through the overhead hatch
- Always wait for assistance before leaving the elevator

Structural collapse

The following is general information for teachers to consider when responding to a structural collapse:

- Drop under or next to sturdy item
- **Cover mouth** with clothing
- **Tap** on a wall or pipe so that rescuers can hear. Use a whistle if one is available.
- Shout only as a **last resort** (shouting can result in the inhalation of dangerous amounts of dust)

Water main breaks

Depending on the severity of a water main break and its location, schools may be closed or kept open with bottled water shipped in. All water fountains are covered and signs are posted in all the bathrooms. Teachers should impress upon students the importance of avoiding the water for drinking and washing.

4.13 Bomb threats

Bomb threats can cause major disruptions to the school day. School administrators will use a threat assessment process, like that described in *Chapter 3: Recognizing warning signs - how can teachers spot a potentially violent student* to determine a proper course of action. The level of response to a threat depends on the specificity of the threat: the more specific the threat (information where the bomb is located, what time it is set to go off, the type of device, etc.), the more administrators will take the threat seriously.

4.13.1 Bomb threat response

In the event of a bomb threat, school and public safety officials may choose from a variety of common response procedures with which teachers should be familiar.

◆ **Search in place**. Areas of the building are scanned for suspicious packages by those most familiar with the layout of the school.
◆ **Evacuation and search**. This option involves school

staff quickly scanning their work area prior to evacuation to a predetermined location. Bomb disposal experts will conduct a second search once the school's occupants are evacuated.

◆ **Sweep of an internal evacuation site, followed by internal evacuation and search**. A bomb sweep is a procedure to locate but not disturb any potential explosive devices. In this procedure, school staff scans their worksites, like in the second option, but evacuate to an *internal* area such as the cafeteria.

Teachers should understand that a bomb can be made to look like virtually any object. Teachers are in many cases more likely to spot an explosive device in familiar areas than a police officer or firefighter. Emergency responders may request aid from teachers when performing a bomb sweep. In this case, teachers should visually sweep the room before leaving if a bomb threat evacuation is called. If they are tasked with sweeping a room, teachers should be sure to do the following:

◆ **Do not touch or disturb anything** – explosive devices can be rigged to detonate when they are moved or disturbed. Instruct students to do the same.
◆ Listen for **unusual sounds**
◆ Divide the room into sections and be sure to scan all areas for anything that seems out of place
◆ Report any unusual items or objects
◆ In rare instances, radios and/or portable phones can

trigger an explosive device. **Do not allow students to use cellular or digital phones**. If a life threatening emergency exists (such as a staff member having a heart attack), however, the risk of setting off an explosive device is much less likely than the risk of death or serious injury that would be present in using a phone or radio to call for help. If a classroom telephone or intercom is present, use it instead.

4.13.2 Information to record

Although teachers do not regularly handle incoming phone calls, they must be prepared for receiving a bomb threat. It is important to record at what **time** the call was taken. The exact **wording** of the threat is very important to determining the threat level. The call's recipient should notice and write down **characteristics** of the caller such as sex, race, age and accent. The caller's voice description is also important (i.e. was he/she laughing/crying, calm/agitated, etc.) as well as any background noises. In many instances, calls may be centered around events such as the day after a student was expelled, major tests, significant anniversary dates, etc. Noting any coinciding events may help identify the perpetrators of a threat.

4.13.3 Questions

Most bomb threats are made by phone. All school staff that have access to a phone should have a list of **questions** next to the phone to be asked in case of a phoned in bomb threat.

1. When is the bomb going to explode?
2. Where is the bomb right now?
3. What kind of bomb is it?
4. What does it look like?
5. Is the bomb in an open container, concealed or disguised?
6. What will cause the bomb to explode?
7. Did you place the bomb?
8. Why did you place the bomb?
9. Where are you calling from?
10. What is your name?
11. What is your address?

This bomb threat information was extracted from *Jane's Workplace Security Handbook.*

4.14 Bombs/explosive devices

While the vast majority of bomb threats are hoaxes, real explosive devices have been placed in schools on more than 60 occasions in recent years according to the Bureau of Alcohol, Tobacco and Firearms (ATF). A bomb can be manufactured to look like or fit within virtually any object, like a purse or a book-bag. Teachers should be aware of the different types of explosives. As possibly the first to encounter them, teachers should know what they look like and how to respond to the various devices. Alertness is therefore key in identifying a potential explosive device in the classroom.

4.14.1 Postal explosive devices

Postal devices are nearly always victim-operated weapons designed to kill an individual for political, personal or ideological reasons. Teachers do not usually receive mail at school that has not been first sorted by others, but they should be aware of recognition and disposal procedures.

What to look for

◆ Unusual balance or shape
◆ Excessive weight for its size
◆ Excessive or unusual wrapping/sealing
◆ Suspicious parts showing, or sticking through the wrapping
◆ Excess postage
◆ No return address when one might be expected
◆ Indications via postmark, return address or other markings that the package comes from an unfamiliar, unexpected or suspicious source
◆ Unusual or overly specific instructions, such as 'open this end first' or a statement that the package should only be opened by a particular individual
◆ Other unusual markings
◆ Similarity to other packages recently reported in the media
◆ Package is identified by x-ray or explosives scanner (if available) as suspect

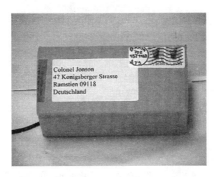

Teachers should know procedures to recognize and dispose of postal explosive devices **2003**/0562513

Response procedures

If a teacher does come into contact with a suspicious package, the following procedures should be followed:

- **NEVER touch, move or open a suspect item**
- Leave the room and evacuate students
- Evacuate to predetermined evacuation sites or internal evacuation site as directed by administration officials,
- Take along emergency response kit
- **Do not** use radios, cellular phones or other electronic devices in the vicinity of the suspect device as in rare circumstances they can set off certain devices
- Call the emergency services and give them information on:

- What the suspect item looks like
- Who has seen or touched the item
- Why it is suspicious
- Where the device located in the facility and how to distinguish it from other items. Provide emergency services with a site map.
- What the room looks like (a sketch diagram of the room could be helpful)
- When the package arrived
- How the package arrived
- When was it first discovered or identified as suspicious
- Who discovered it or identified it
- If there is any known reason why someone sent the bomb
- What search, evacuation or shelter-in-place measures have been implemented

Bomb found in locker

- **Do not touch, move, inspect or disturb alleged bomb**
- Turn off all "walkie-talkie" radios and cell phones
- Secure area around locker and use fixed-line communications (i.e. PA system) to advise appropriate people (i.e. administrators, emergency responders)
- Evacuate students if directed to do so
- Leave classroom door unlocked
- Teachers take attendance of students at evacuation point

4.14.2 Firebombs/incendiary devices

Firebombs and incendiary devices are commonly used to create an immediate, intense fire and are usually used against a building or a vehicle. When combined with other hazards, such as fuel storage tanks, they present a significant danger to a building.

What to look for

◆ Glass or plastic containers filled with a flammable or incendiary mixture

◆ Glass bottle devices with a dry chemical mixture strapped to the side or fuse (such as a rag) coming from the top

◆ Plastic bottle device with a liquid-acid filled glove and a bag of dry chemicals

◆ Any other collection of materials that could cause a fire found in a vulnerable or unusual place

Warning

◆ *Certain incendiaries may react violently or even explode if water is used to fight the fire*

◆ *Multiple incendiaries are sometimes used to create a larger fire. If one device is found, emergency response personnel will usually check for others.*

Response procedures

It may be helpful for teachers to be familiar with the following generic procedures to an incident involving incendiary devices:

◆ **NEVER touch or move a suspected incendiary item**
◆ If directed to do so, evacuate students from the building using standard procedures. Evacuate to the farthest predetermined evacuation site, or as far away as possible as directed by emergency response personnel who will determine a safe distance.
◆ Take attendance upon completing evacuation
◆ Make sure to bring emergency response kit
◆ **Do no**t use radios, cellular phones or other electronic devices in the vicinity of the suspect device as they can set off certain devices. Control the use of students' cell phones and electronic devices.
◆ The emergency services will need to know the following information:
  ● What the suspect item looks like
  ● Who has seen or touched the item
  ● Why it is suspicious
  ● Where in the facility is the device located and how to distinguish it from other items. Provide emergency services with a site map.
  ● What the room looks like (a sketch diagram of the room could be helpful)
  ● When the device was found
  ● How the device was found

- When it was first discovered or identified as suspicious
- Who discovered or identified it
- Any known reason why someone placed a device there
- What evacuation measures have been implemented

4.14.3 Package bombs

It is recommended that teachers vigilantly control items that enter the classroom and look for items that do not belong. Effective control procedures can significantly reduce the possibility of a bomb planted inside the school's premises. Teachers should, however, be prepared in case one gets through.

Package bombs vary in size and sophistication from small homemade pipe bombs to complex luggage bombs with multiple detonators. Pipe bombs are normally placed near doors and windows to cause immediate damage to the facility and the people using that facility. Larger explosive devices are usually aimed at crowded areas and are intended to create a sense of fear and panic as well as casualties.

A bomb in a facility may operate on a timer, be detonated by the actions of the victim (lifting an item or opening it) or by radio control (less likely).

What to look for

Explosive devices are often concealed inside common items such as briefcases or backpacks, or hidden in a trashcan or box to disguise them during transport and placement. Teachers should look out for the following:

◆ An abandoned common item (backpack, purse, etc.)
◆ A person seen to leave an item behind deliberately
◆ An item that looks out of place in its surroundings
◆ Metal or PVC pipe with caps screwed onto each end
◆ Fuse/detonator (may not be apparent from the outside)
◆ Nails or screws may be imbedded within or fastened to the outside of a device

Warning
◆ *Never pick-up or move a suspect item. Bombers will often hide pipe bombs in bags, backpacks, trashcans or boxes.*

Response procedures
Teachers should follow the response procedures as determined by their schools when responding to a suspected explosive device. The following is a generic response protocol for responding to an incident involving a package bomb:

◆ **NEVER touch or move a suspect item**
◆ Leave the room AND close the door, evacuating students and staff from room
◆ **Do not** use radios, cellular phones or other electronic devices in the vicinity of the suspect device as they can set off certain devices. Instruct students to do the same.

◆ Notify administrators and emergency services
◆ The emergency services will want to know the following information:
  ● What the suspect item looks like
  ● Who has seen or touched the item
  ● Why it is suspicious
  ● Where the item is located and how to distinguish it from other items. Provide emergency services with a site map.
  ● What does the room look like (a sketch diagram of the room could be helpful)
  ● When the item was found
  ● How the item was found
  ● When was it first discovered or identified as suspicious
  ● Who discovered or identified it
  ● Any known reason why someone placed a bomb there
  ● What search, evacuation or shelter-in-place measures have been implemented
◆ If directed to do so, evacuate students using standard procedures. Evacuate as far away as possible until emergency response personnel determine a safe distance. Take attendance of students.
◆ If directed to do so, shelter-in-place
  ● Put at least two solid walls (not cubicle or thin walls) between the device and those on-scene
  ● Keep everyone away from doorways. Blast pressure can be maintained for longer when channeled down

a corridor or hallway than if in an open space.

● Keep people away from windows, mirrors, glass and other materials that could break and become dangerous fragments due to an explosion

4.14.4 Vehicle bombs

Although large bombs, such as vehicle bombs, can destroy the inside of a school building, teachers will probably not notice them from inside the classroom. When outside the building, for example during recess, teachers may be able to spot suspiciously parked or moving vehicles. Once identified, it is the teacher's responsibility for managing classroom evacuation if they are directed to so.

What to look for

Teachers should look for suspicious vehicles in which explosives are generally concealed in order to transport them to the target location.

◆ Vehicles that appear to be heavily loaded and hastily abandoned at a high-threat site
◆ Vehicle may be newly painted or feature new fiberglass, epoxies or caulking
◆ Strange smells may emanate from the suspect vehicle
◆ On a cargo-type truck or van, the back doors may be welded shut or have new, additional padlocks

Warning

◆ *Time is critical due to the massive destructive power of these devices. Evacuation must be quick. Keep as many buildings and walls as possible between students and the suspect device during evacuation. Buildings will channel a blast down open streets.*

◆ *Be aware of underground gas lines and above-ground fuel storage points or fuel stations in the blast area. They will be affected in a blast.*

Response procedures

The following is a generic checklist to consider when responding to an incident involving a vehicle bomb:

◆ **NEVER touch or move a suspect vehicle**

◆ **Do not** use radios, cellular phones or other electronic devices in the vicinity of the suspect device as they can set off certain detonators. Instruct students to do the same.

◆ Notify school administrators and emergency services

◆ Evacuate students from the building if directed to do so. Evacuate to as far away as possible until emergency response personnel determine a safe distance. Take attendance of students

◆ If directed to do so, shelter-in-place
  ● Put at least two solid walls between the device and those on-scene
  ● Keep everyone away from doorways. Blast pressure can be maintained for longer when channeled down a corridor or hallway than if in an open space

- Keep people away from windows and other flying glass hazards

This bombs/explosive devices information is based on that developed in *Jane's Unconventional Weapons Response Handbook* and *Jane's Workplace Security Handbook*.

4.15 Chemical and biological incidents

The October 2001 mailings of anthrax-tainted letters and the reported plans by Al Qaeda to use a crop duster to disperse chemical or biological agents have contributed to an increasing public awareness of chemical/biological weapons. Governments are allocating billions of dollars to increase preparedness for chemical and biological attacks. Schools, potential soft targets for terrorism, should do their part to enhance response capacity to these low probability but high consequence events. Teachers are on the front lines and must be prepared to respond to a chemical/biological attack. Minutes count; a swift response, for which teachers can play a part, can save lives.

Action steps in the emergency operations plan will typically use such measures as sheltering-in-place, evacuation, mass decontamination of victims and the rapid establishment of exclusion zones (zones that limit access to a disaster site). It is especially important for teachers to be familiar with how to perform each functional protocol along with specific response protocols for chemical/biological weapons.

4.15.1 What to look for

Even though chemical/biological attacks have been a rare occurrence, it may be necessary for teachers to recognize symptoms in groups of students or school staff to limit potential damage to a school. Since most chemical weapons will produce immediate symptoms in victims, a chemical attack is typically noticed close to the site and time of the attack. The initial response is likely to be made by emergency response personnel who are summoned to the vicinity of the attack(s).

Unlike a chemical attack, the use of a biological weapon may not be immediately apparent; indications typically begin to appear over a greater period of time and often in places remote from the actual attack site. The identification of a biological attack is more likely to involve medical and public health officials and a coordinated public health surveillance network.

Teachers should be aware of the following symptoms that may help identify a chemical/biological attack:

- ◆ Unexplained casualties
  - ● Multiple victims
  - ● Serious illnesses
  - ● Nausea, disorientation, difficulty breathing, convulsions
  - ● Definite casualty patterns
- ◆ Unusual dead or dying animals
- ◆ Unusual liquid, spray or vapor

- ● Droplets, oily film
- ● Unexplained odor
- ● Low flying clouds/fog unrelated to weather
- ◆ Suspicious devices/packages
  - ● Unusual metal debris
  - ● Abandoned spray devices
  - ● Unexplained munitions
- ◆ Unusual swarm or lack of insects

4.15.2 Response procedures

As chemical attacks – particularly those involving fast-acting nerve agents – produce more rapid onset of symptoms, the emergency medical response must be immediate and effective to minimize the severity of the harmful effects on victims. As in many cases, teachers are "first-responders" and must be aware of procedures that can limit the exposure of harmful substances to themselves and their students.

Teachers can also help responders quickly identify the likely agent used to facilitate more effective emergency medical care. If teachers can provide an accurate description of symptoms and physical reactions of those that are sick, then responders and the public health community can work more quickly to determine the cause and cure.

It is important that teachers understand how the emergency services will respond to a chemical/biological incident. This knowledge will reduce confusion and panic among teachers and others affected and therefore should improve the efficiency and effectiveness of the response. The following guidelines provide an overview for school personnel of what to do in the event of such an incident.

On arrival at the scene, emergency response personnel will establish site boundaries that may enlarge or shrink depending on the weather (for instance if the wind changes direction) or the agent becomes known and a different site size is warranted. **Emergency response personnel will give instructions on the safest course of action**. This may involve evacuation or shelter-in-place.

Teachers should know the following procedures if they suspect a chemical/biological attack:

- **Notify the school administration and inform emergency services**
- **Always follow instructions from emergency services personnel**
- **Contain** the area. If possible, seal off the area in which the release is suspected, closing all doors and windows and shutting down the heating, ventilating, and air conditioning (HVAC) system.
- **Evacuate** students to a pre-determined location if directed to do so. Ideally this should be **uphill**, **upwind** and at least 300 ft (90 m) from the facility. Ensure all doors and windows are closed after the evacuation.
- **Shelter-in-place** if directed to do so. If this is directed, ignore other response procedures until directed to evacuate.

◆ **Separate** those who were exposed to the suspected release from those who were not. The exposed individuals should remain at least 50 ft (15 m) from the main group (upwind and uphill). **Avoiding cross-contamination through separation is critical.** For example, in an anthrax incident, those exposed will be decontaminated and receive antibiotics first, significantly improving their chance of survival.

◆ Victims should be placed outside, in a breeze if possible, if they have been contaminated by vapors. Have victims remove their outer clothing.

◆ If contamination remains on victims, emergency response personnel will flush victims with water and/or a hypochlorite and water solution, according to local procedures and protocols. Before emergency responders arrive, it may be necessary to follow procedures detailed in *Section 4.15.3 Personal decontamination procedures.*

◆ **Wait** and ensure that all students involved remain on-scene until the emergency services arrive. This helps prevent the spread of further contamination from the incident site to other locations such as hospitals.

◆ **Reassure** students that help is on the way. Watch for and treat signs of **shock.**

◆ **No student who is able to walk and talk is in immediate danger of loss of life**

◆ In any chemical/biological incident, there will be **panic** and possibly hysteria. **Managing panic** is a key step in safely resolving a critical incident. Teachers should provide comfort and reassurance for affected students.

The chemical-biological section is based on procedures found in *Jane's Chem-Bio Handbook.*

Suspicious letter/powder

If a teacher receives a letter in the mail that, when opened, contained a substance such as dust, powder, cream or liquid, he/she should take the following procedures:

◆ Immediately isolate the letter and contents
◆ Be careful not to breathe or touch the substance
◆ Leave the letter where it is, clear the room of all people and students and close the door to the room
◆ Anyone in the room should wash their hands with soap, water and a small amount of bleach
◆ If the substance was inhaled, blow nose and save the tissue in a plastic bag
◆ If the substance gets on clothing, change clothes and bag the used clothing in a plastic bag
◆ Call school administration and emergency services

4.15.3 Personal decontamination procedures

In case of possible contamination by a vapor chemical agent, teachers should evacuate students from the area, preferably into the wind. They should wait for additional medical support if instructed to do so by emergency responders. In case of a possible contamination by a liquid chemical agent, it is advisable to follow these procedures immediately:

◆ Immediately withdraw from the area where contamination occurred. Evacuate building or shelter-in-place depending on direction by emergency services

   ◆ If contaminates are visible on skin, use the brush and blot method:

     ● Immediately brush off agent with a blunt object (stick, edge of book, etc.)

     ● Use absorbent material to soak up agent (soap detergent, dirt, flour, etc.)

◆ After visible agent has been removed from skin, remove clothing and continue

     ● Chemical removal: decontaminate skin using copious amounts of soap and water

     ● Physical removal: flush with water if possible; use dirt, flour or whatever absorbent material is available, according to local emergency procedures and protocols

◆ Put on clean clothing (paper gowns)

◆ Always follow directions from emergency services and public health personnel

Beware of victims – some victims may become agitated and fearful and may attempt to either leave the exclusion zone or approach, or even contact, rescue personnel. Victims must be contained if risk of further contamination is to be prevented.

This chemical-biological information was extracted from *Jane's Chem-Bio Handbook.*

4.16 Nuclear and radiological incidents

The U.S. Department of Justice announced in June 2002 the arrest of a suspected al Qaeda member who allegedly planned to detonate a radiological dispersal device (RDD), or dirty bomb, in Washington, DC. This arrest has raised public awareness (and fear) of the threat posed by nuclear and radiological weapons. Managing the fear generated by a nuclear or radiological incident can be just as important as preventing casualties. Teachers should expect fear and panic by students in reaction to an incident even when the school is not in immediate danger. There will be an immediate urge to leave school and return home; however, this reaction could lead to other casualties if evacuation is not yet warranted. Managing that fear and reacting effectively is essential.

4.16.1 Radiological weapons

Radiation is invisible, odorless and tasteless. The recognition of a radiological attack after a device has detonated is complicated by the delayed onset of radiological symptoms, if they occur at all. Without the use of radiological detection equipment, recognizing a radiological attack is difficult unless there have been verbal threats, warnings or other such indicators.

An attack with radiological weapons, or "dirty" weapons, is much more likely than from nuclear weapons. Press reports in December 2003 indicate that radiological weapons may have reached the black market from stocks in the former Soviet Union in Moldova. This is an area of high concern and has increased the possibility that radiological weapons may be used.

The following are the three main types of radiological weapons:

♦   **Radiological Dispersal Devices** (RDDs), also known as **dirty bombs**, use conventional explosives to spread or disperse radiological material

 ●   RDDs are capable of causing considerable radiation contamination and are a **serious health hazard**

 ●   While the conventional explosives used in an RDD would cause casualties and structural damage, radiological experts believe it is **doubtful a RDD would generate immediate radiation-related deaths**

 ●   The limited delivery area of RDDs means the radiation **would not kill large numbers of people**. The effects would depend on the **type** and **amount** of radioactive material used.

 ●   If undetected and untreated, it could take days, months or years for an RDD to cause radiation casualties. This is particularly true in urban areas, where building materials such as concrete would provide some shielding.

♦   **Simple Radiological Dispersal** (SRD), the most basic form of radiological weapon, is the deliberate spreading of radioactive material by, for example:

- Adding radioactive material to food or water supplies to cause **radiation poisoning**
- Placement in an envelope and mailed to a specific person (much like the October 2001 anthrax attacks in the U.S.)
- Radioactive sources planted or placed in a target area with the intent of exposing persons to high radioactive doses
- ◆ **Simple Radiological Dispersal Devices** (SRDD) are created by combining radioactive material with a non-explosive scattering device, such as a fan or atomizer

What to look for

Teachers should be aware of general indicators that radiological contamination may have occurred, including the following symptoms:

- ◆ **Unusual numbers of sick or dying people:**
  - General symptoms of radiation sickness include nausea, vomiting, diarrhea, fatigue, weakness, fever, reddened skin and headaches
  - Casualties may happen hours, days or weeks after an incident
  - Time elapsed between exposure and appearance of symptoms depends on the radioactive material used and the dose received
- ◆ Unusual **metal debris, unexplained devices** or munitions-like material
- ◆ **Radiation symbols** on container labels

- ◆ **Heat-emitting material** without any visible energy source
- ◆ **Glowing material or particles** (radio luminescence, colored residue)

Response procedures

Teachers should follow the emergency response plan for their school and directions of emergency response personnel in the event of a radiological release. As with other mass incapacitating attacks, however, teachers should be prepared with the following information if contact with these officials is not possible.

If the presence of a RDD is suspected, **pre-blast** response procedures should be similar to those for a **suspected bomb** (see *4.13 Bombs/explosive devices* for more information). The **radiological impacts** should be considered **secondary to the impacts of the explosive** device when lives are at risk.

After any nuclear or radiological incident, the goal is to keep radiation exposure **as low as possible**. Keep in mind four exposure factors:

- ◆ **Time**: reduce the duration of exposure
- ◆ **Distance**: increase distance from the radiation source
- ◆ **Shielding**: place shielding between yourself and the source
- ◆ **Quantity**: limit the quantity of radiation (reduce contamination)

The decision to evacuate or shelter-in-place during a radiological incident is simpler than for a nuclear incident. Most experts believe that the shielding afforded by concrete buildings is more effective than increasing distance from the incident site, making shelter-in-place a good choice. **Always follow the directions of emergency response personnel,** however. If a teacher must make a decision in a crisis situation, they should keep the following factors in mind:

◆ **Evacuate students from the building** using standard procedures
  ● If **directed** to do so by emergency response personnel
  ● If the **threat of fire or structural collapse** outweighs radiation factors. For example, if the building was the target of a large bomb that incorporated radioactive materials (as with an RDD). Immediate life concerns should come before radiation in a nuclear or radiological incident.
  ● If a suspected radiological weapon is found **in the building** (could be a very small device)
  ● **Always evacuate into the wind and away** from the suspected point of origin of the explosion
  ● **Cover nose and mouth** with a cloth to prevent inhalation of radioactive particles
◆ **Shelter-in-place**
  ● If **directed** to do so by emergency response personnel
  ● Large bombs, such as those possibly used as an

RDD, can cause extensive damage to buildings. Shelter-in-place decisions should be made **only if the building is still sound and provides protection**. If the building is on fire or on the verge of collapse, evacuate immediately.

- Send students to **an underground area** such as a basement or shelter, if possible. Close all doors to areas of possible contamination. The ground and concrete of the building should provide some shielding against radiation.

- Use **decontamination procedures** (below) if dust from the explosion has entered the building or if people are coming in from the outside

- If **inhalation or ingestion** is suspected **immediate medical care at a hospital** may be required. Coordinate efforts with local emergency medical services and public health department.

Decontamination procedures

Contamination occurs when radioactive materials cling to exposed body and clothing surfaces, are breathed in or consumed in food or water. **External contamination** is dealt with through decontamination procedures, which when done rapidly can be effective. Changing clothes under controlled conditions can remove up to 95 percent of external contaminants.

- **Remove clothing** and place in a tightly sealed plastic bag for disposal

◆ **Shower entire body**, including hair, with copious amounts soap and water followed by a water rinse
◆ Put on **clean clothes**
◆ Follow up with **medical personnel** to ensure decontamination
◆ Individuals with **internal contamination** require specialized medical treatment.

It is important to remember that immediate life concerns should come before radiation concerns in a nuclear or radiological incident. The **threat of fire, structural collapse or other imminent danger** outweighs radiation factors.

Warning

◆ *Separate those exposed to the suspected release from those who were not*
◆ *If teachers are unsure of the best course of action, it may be best to **close doors, windows, shut down the HVAC system and elevators and remain in place** until guidance from the emergency services is given (for example if your facility is downwind of the incident site)*

4.16.2 Nuclear weapons

Nuclear weapons are the least likely, yet potentially most devastating, means of terrorist attack. They would most likely be used on high-value, symbolic targets in urban areas and not likely to be directed at schools. Schools near high-value targets, however, may be in the blast radius or the fall-out zone.

What to look for

A nuclear detonation is recognizable for the following characteristics:

- **Intense light** lasting 1–10 seconds
- **Thermal pulse:** flash fires, blindness if the light is viewed directly, skin burns of varying severity depending on distance from blast, can occur
- **Blast wave:** a shock wave whose force and effects decrease with distance from point of origin (first leveled buildings, then felled trees, then only shattered windows)
- **Electromagnetic pulse:** disabled electronic equipment, including cars, radios, computers and telephones
- **Visual effects:** mushroom cloud or other large plume at the point of origin
- **Radiation:** the highest doses will be present at the blast site, although contaminated fallout can travel great distances

Response procedures

Teachers should follow the school guidelines and directions from emergency response officials for dealing with a nuclear blast. Certain steps can increase survival. The following steps are not foolproof. There are reports of people surviving nuclear blasts by taking similar actions, however. At first notice of a nuclear weapon detonation (usually intense bright light or a warning signal), teachers should do the following, and instruct students to do the same beforehand because there will be no time to give instructions:

- Immediately **look away** from the light and close eyes
- **Drop** to the ground or floor
- Immediately get away from windows and behind **cover** (a wall, a ditch, a desk, a stairwell below street level, anything outside the line-of-sight to the explosion)
- **Cover exposed skin**
- **Cover nose and mouth with cloth** to prevent particles from being inhaled
- **Wait** until blast wave passes and debris stops falling
- **Check for injury**
- Once the blast has passed and debris has stopped falling, decide whether to evacuate or shelter-in-place

The decision to evacuate or shelter-in-place during a nuclear incident is a difficult one and likely will not be made by teachers. In case school administrators or emergency response personnel are incapacitated or not able to be contacted, teachers should be aware of the following considerations. Factors such as the distance from the blast site and the size of device will influence that decision. Even so, many experts disagree on the best course of action. If shelter provides adequate protection and distance from the blast site is moderate, it may be wise to shelter-in-place to avoid further radiation contamination. Immediate evacuation is required if there is threat of a firestorm (a massive fire). The need to reduce the duration of radiation exposure and to increase the distance from the highly radioactive blast site is also a consideration. If the school is located directly in the fallout of the blast, it is advisable to evacuate immediately.

Always **follow the directions of emergency response personnel,** but if they are not available, teachers should make a **decision** to **evacuate** or **shelter-in-place** based on the following factors:

- ◆ **Evacuate students** using standard procedures
  - ● **If directed** to do so by emergency response personnel
  - ● If **adequate transportation or evacuation routes** are still functioning and accessible
  - ● If the **threat of fire or structural collapse** outweighs radiation factors
  - ● The school is located directly in the fallout of the blast
  - ● If there is an immediate need to reduce the duration of radiation exposure and to increase the distance from the highly radioactive blast site
  - ● Evacuate students **into the wind and away** from the suspected explosion site
  - ● **Cover nose and mouth** with a cloth to prevent inhalation of radioactive particles and ensure that students do the same
- ◆ If evacuation is not possible or safe, or if emergency personnel direct, **shelter-in-place**
  - ● Shelter-in-place decisions should be made **only if the building is still sound, provides protection and is a moderate distance from the blast site**. If the building is on fire or on the verge of collapse, evacuate immediately.

- Move students to an **underground area** such as a basement or shelter and close all doors to areas of possible contamination. The ground and concrete structure of the building should provide some protection against radiation.
- Use **decontamination procedures** (above) if dust from the explosion has entered the building or if people are coming in from the outside
- If **inhalation or ingestion** is suspected, **seek immediate specialized medical care**

This nuclear and radiological weapons information is based on that contained in *Jane's Unconventional Weapons Response Handbook*.

NOTES

Chapter 5

After a traumatic event – how do teachers help students recover?

5.1 Introduction

A traumatic event is a sudden and shocking experience in which there is injury, death or the serious threat of harm. Powerful emotional and physical reactions are common after a major traumatic incident. Terror, helplessness and horror are the primary response to a life threat, like those 8,000 students and staff experienced of the schools near the former World Trade Center on September 11, 2001.

These emotions are difficult to overcome. Although teachers can do a great deal to help their students, changes in classroom behavior are unavoidable. It does not matter if the traumatic event is a large scale danger like a tornado or terrorist attack, or a private trauma, such as a student suicide, car accident or child abuse. In either situation, children and adolescents need the help of trusted adults to learn to cope constructively with their confusion, fear and distress or, in some cases, to obtain professional help.

It is very likely that any traumatic event a student or teacher experiences will have an effect on the classroom. The teacher may be the first to recognize the symptoms of trauma when the student's behavior changes and who must find new ways to re-engage the student in classroom activities and learning.

Teachers will not be alone in helping students to recover after an emergency situation. **Crisis intervention teams** (CITs)

---

can assist in restoring the learning environment in a variety of ways. These efforts include providing **psychological first aid, comfort and emotional support** to school victims of violence. CIT work begins when law enforcement and other emergency personnel have secured and deemed the affected area to be safe and continues until every child or staff member that has been traumatized by the event has had his/her individual needs met.

Chapter overview

This chapter will approach the following topics on post-trauma recovery procedures and resources:

♦ Students reactions to a traumatic event
♦ Recovery procedures
♦ Teacher recovery/burnout
♦ Recovery resources

5.2 Student reactions to a traumatic event

Although there is presently a great deal of concern about terrorism, most students are traumatized as victims or witnesses to child abuse, domestic violence, school or community violence, as well as natural or human-caused disasters. These incidents all include serious threats of bodily harm before, during and after school.

Traumatic incidents produce age-specific reactions in students. The following are descriptions of how young

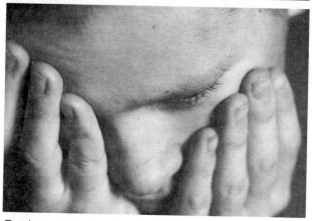

Teachers may be the first to recognize symptoms of trauma in students
2003/0562498

children, older elementary and middle school students and adolescents react to traumatic stress:

♦ The **younger the child,** the more likely that he/she will feel completely helpless after violence or disaster. Crying and clinging behavior reflects a wish to be protected and reassured.

♦ **Older elementary and middle school students** may feel helpless, but they may begin to think of ways to escape, combat or confront the situation. Unlike younger children, they may feel guilty for "failing" to act or ashamed that they were not of help to adults in danger. Not all of their ideas may be appropriate or constructive and can result in overly aggressive or confused and intemperate reactions.

◆ **Adolescents** can place themselves in danger as they begin to engage in more adult activities, such as driving cars and going to parties where there may be alcohol and drugs. Poor judgment and impulsive behaviors can create dangerous situations before and after a traumatic event. Intense guilt after a severe crisis can lead to increased risk-taking behaviors, including reckless driving, unwise sexual activity and increased substance use and abuse.

5.2.1 Symptoms of child trauma

In the classroom or on campus, children and adolescents may exhibit the following behaviors after a traumatic event:

Actions/feelings

◆ **Preschool and young elementary school**
- Feeling helpless
- Experiencing paralyzing and generalized fear
- Acting confused
- Unable to talk about fears and concerns
- Engaging in traumatic play, as in reenacting the incident repeatedly

◆ **Older elementary and middle school**
- Facing traumatic reminders of the violent acts that cause additional fears
- Telling and retelling details of the traumatic event

- Reenacting the incident or playing games that include some type of trauma
- Being afraid of being overwhelmed by their feelings
- Acting in hostile, aggressive and/or bullying ways toward friends, neighbors and classmates

- **Adolescents**
  - Detachment, denial and/or guilt
  - Shame about their fear and vulnerability, fearing their peers and youth culture would disapprove

Change in habits
- **Preschool and young elementary school**
  - Showing regressive symptoms, such as thumb-sucking, bed-wetting and baby talk (in young children only)
  - Experiencing sleeping problems including nightmares
  - Having eating problems, including loss of appetite or refusal to eat

- **Older elementary and middle school**
  - Having trouble eating with an upset stomach or little appetite
  - Having trouble sleeping and/or having night scares, such as a fear of ghosts
  - Being afraid of routine things: being alone, going to certain places, going to sleep

- Doing things they did when they were younger: thumb-sucking, sleeping with parents, clinging to teachers and parents

◆ **Adolescents**
  - New or increased risk-taking or life-threatening behavior, such as drug or alcohol abuse, promiscuous sexual behavior, criminal or delinquent acts, traffic violations
  - Regressive behavior, such as thumb-sucking, sleeping with parents, clinging to teachers and parents
  - Abrupt changes in friendship or abandonment of friendships
  - Adult behavior, such as becoming pregnant, leaving school, marrying

View of the world
◆ **Preschool and young elementary school**
  - Showing separation anxiety, such as clinging behavior and fear of being alone, difficulty being away from parents or worrying about when parents will return

◆ **Older elementary and middle school**
  - Worrying that something bad might happen to parent(s), caretaker(s), sister(s) and brother(s) and other close family and friends

◆ **Adolescents**
  ● New fears or worries such as something bad might happen to parent(s), caretaker(s), sister(s) and brother(s) and/or other close family and friends

Source: *Jane's Citizen's Safety Guide*

To support the teacher in the classroom, school mental health professionals (school counselors, psychologists and social workers) should establish and familiarize teachers with a referral process for student counseling. Teachers should become familiar with the referral process that each school or school district has in place. Early detection of emotional distress and referral for school intervention services improves the student's prognosis for recovery.

5.2.2 Three main components of post-traumatic stress

A tornado, earthquake or act of violence may sweep across a city in a few minutes, but the emotional devastation can continue long after the disaster is over. People who go through a natural disaster, school shooting, or terrorist attack feel that "everything changes." Intense physical and emotional reactions continue around three clusters of post-traumatic stress symptoms:

1. **Students may continue to re-experience the event.** They may have repeated upsetting images or "flashbacks" to what they saw or heard. This may occur

involuntarily during the day in class or at night through interrupted sleep or nightmares. In either situation, students' classroom concentration is poor and their ability to think clearly is impaired.

2. **Students may attempt to avoid people or places that remind them of the traumatic event**. If the event occurred at school or during the school day, then going to school or being in school may in itself be a "traumatic reminder." A drop in student attendance is a common outcome after school shootings or after a terrorist attack such as the bombing of the Murrah Federal Building in Oklahoma City.

3. **Students may continue to experience physical symptoms connected with the trauma**. They may have trouble sleeping and become irritable. They may have difficulty controlling their emotions, becoming easily angered or upset. They may become "jumpy," startle easily at noises and be excessively alert for new danger. Sometimes, stomach aches or headaches become more frequent. Engaging the assistance of the school nurse can help to identify somatic complaints as part of the trauma response as opposed to a physical illness.

5.3 Recovery procedures

Because of the close bond teachers often form with students, they are in a powerful position to help students deal with trauma and tragedy. Teachers will find it helpful to know basic strategies to assist students coping with powerful and uncontrollable emotions. Teachers should also be aware of the effects of trauma on themselves and other adults in the school as well as parents. The reactions of the entire school community will affect a school's recovery.

5.3.1 Helping students cope

When students have been traumatized, teachers can use the following strategies to help students cope with traumatic stress:

Activities

♦   Make time available after class or during a conference period for student(s) who are having emotional difficulty. Listening and understanding is "good medicine."

♦   Plan a lesson that helps students to put the disaster or tragedy into perspective and provides a calm environment for sharing thoughts and feelings

♦   Help students identify and plan constructive activities that will improve human relations or conditions at school or in the community

♦   Encourage students to write or draw their feelings and their ideas for change

♦   Practice the safety measures to be taken in future disasters

Approach to the students

♦   Be prepared for some outbursts. Acknowledge that everyone is under more stress. Defuse the anger if possible until the student is calm enough to talk on a one-to-one basis.

◆ Be patient and encourage the student to relax with simple relaxation techniques such as deep breathing, muscle relaxation, or using positive imagery. These can be practiced prior to test-taking, class presentations, etc.

◆ Reaffirm the future. Be a good role model in the face of adversity.

◆ Be a role model for the expression of thoughts, feelings and actions

◆ Reassure them that things will improve over time

◆ Help students get counseling, if needed

Intervention

When a student cannot seem to calm down and is having an especially difficult time, teachers can take the following measures:

◆ If a student exhibits disruptive behavior, determine if he/she is experiencing one or more of the three components of traumatic stress

◆ Ask if the student is having interrupted sleep or sufficient sleep

◆ Explain that traumatic stress can dramatically change emotions, thinking and behavior

◆ Refer the student to the counselor, school nurse or both

◆ Help the student to accept the referral without any shame or blame

◆   Follow-up with a parent conference to express concern.
     Having the school counselor join the conference will
     underscore the importance of getting help for the
     student.

Social support is critical to managing stress. Caring and
supportive relationships in the classroom buffer the impact of
stressful emotions or crises. Avoiding discussions of
distressing events is not helpful.

Caring adults, such as parents and teachers, may think that
children are not bothered by an event or believe that a
discussion of the event will be upsetting to the child. This
often happens when children are pressured to talk "on
demand." Letting students know, however, that a caring adult
is available to listen to their thoughts and feelings gives them
permission to begin the problem solving process. Adults who
emphasize the need to maintain tight control over emotions
miss the opportunity to provide needed support and to help
students cope with the trauma.

5.3.2 Stages of recovery for adults

Five stages of recovery have frequently been observed in
adults after most disasters and acts of mass violence.

Initial phase

This is a period of shock and disbelief during which people
feel numb and disoriented. The most frequently asked
question is why the disaster occurred, why it "had to happen"

or, after an act of human malice, why people would perpetrate such an act on innocent victims. Anger and outrage may quickly follow.

Heroic phase

During this phase, a community celebrates law enforcement, emergency workers and other "heroes" during a brief period of intense media attention. Community members, teachers and other staff will step forward as well to mobilize the resources needed to recover from an incident.

Honeymoon phase

This stage develops as survivors express the determination to do everything they can to overcome the tragedy. This phase may involve rescue efforts and a surge of goodwill and assistance from a community. New alliances and relation-ships are formed and the community and school are open to positive change.

Disillusionment phase

During this phase, the community or country's attention may turn away from the event. The rescue efforts may be at an end. The survivors of the school and community are left with the real impact of trauma and loss. The inspirational stories begin to evolve into the difficult reality of grief, loss and frustration. After an earthquake or a tornado, the rebuilding of schools and homes may be a long and difficult process. After a school shooting or terrorist attack, real life problems continue in addition to the adversity faced by the traumatic event. Pre-existing conflicts and problems that seemed resolved return. High expectations are disappointed; dis-illusionment with authority figures, caretakers, family members and others are common experiences.

Rebuilding phase

This phase begins in earnest when some progress is made in re-establishing a "new normal." Life may not be restored to what it was before the traumatic event, but there are signs of hope and recovery.

5.3.3 Stages of recovery for children

The process of recovery for children is made complex by the factors of the child's age, developmental maturity and life experience. In addition, children's recoveries are linked to parents' reactions and recovery, and the parents' attention to their children's needs. Parents need to serve as role models in assessing and coping with their own traumatic experiences. Children learn best by example.

Research has also shown that parents may not be aware of the effects of traumatic stress on their children, either because they underestimate the psychological effects or because they may not know about an incident that occurred outside the home. Often, it is the teacher who notices the change in a student's ability to think, reason, and cope with peers at school.

The posttraumatic stress reactions of children and adolescents can be mild or severe. They may last for a brief time or for many years. The reactions can also get worse during certain periods of the child's life.

Anniversary dates, such as birthdays of lost friends or loved ones, holidays, or the date of the incident, such as a school shooting, may trigger strong emotional reactions that require additional classroom support and renewed referrals to school or community mental health professionals.

When students experience traumatic stress, teachers should take the following measures:

- Acknowledge the seriousness of the traumatic event
- Encourage them to ask for help when they experience traumatic reminders
- Let them know that emotional support and understanding is available but that disruptive or hurtful behavior will not be tolerated

The grieving process

Dealing with the tragedy of losing a loved one can make students have even more complex and fearful emotions. Having them list what they are thinking and feeling is critical for them to heal and for a teacher to be aware of their well-being. Teachers can tell children it is OK to feel bad and that they are not alone by sharing emotions.

Explain there is a grieving process that includes similar feelings for both children and adults. A child may first experience disbelief that may turn into anger. This reaction helps them distance themselves from the loss. Even with little or no hope for a recovery, they may tell themselves that they can do something to solve the problem. Feelings of regret or responsibility from past incidents (no matter how small or big) may allow children to believe the situation can improve. Sooner or later, sadness and crying occurs as the child begins to understand that life needs to continue without the person. Depending on the child, he or she may feel forgiveness and a sense of peace about what happened for the first time. The child may still feel sad but has stopped trying to fight reality.

5.3.4 Working with mental health professionals/ school counselors

Teachers cannot and should not be placed in the role of being a mental health counselor. School counselors, psychologists and social workers are the "front line" referral resources for teachers who identify students experiencing traumatic stress. Although the teacher may recognize changes in a student's mood or behavior, it is the school or community mental health professional that can best provide intervention services to the student and his/her family.

5.3.5 Working with parents and the community

Parents are essential to the recovery of children, but may not have the basic information to assist and support their children after disasters and violent incidents. If a teacher suspects that a student has been traumatized, a good first step is to help parents learn as much as they can about child traumatic

---

stress. Teachers can work with the school counselor, psychologist or social worker to increase parental awareness through individual conferences or parent workshops conducted by the school nurse, the school mental health professional or by a representative from a community child guidance clinic.

Studies have shown that parents who are well informed about their child's feelings and behavior can contribute materially to their child's emotional health and school performance. Parents who misinterpret misbehavior caused by traumatic stress often mistakenly respond with criticism and disciplinary action, compounding the child's stress. What is crucial is that parents allow time for their children to express difficult emotions in a safe and caring home environment. The teacher's role is to help parents understand the special needs of children who are experiencing traumatic stress.

Special attention should be paid to providing information and assistance in the parent's native language. If possible, teachers may try to arrange a translator to be present at a parent conference or workshop. Reaching out to churches, social clubs, and youth organizations is also beneficial to both parents and students.

5.4 Teacher recovery/burnout

When traumatic incidents affect a school, students are not the only individuals who must recover under difficult situations. Teachers suffer many of the same types of traumatic

Teacher burnout can happen after witnessing repeated traumatic incidents

2003/0564537

experiences, losses and secondary stresses as students. Teachers are expected, however, to bounce back more quickly to set an example and support the recovery of students. This is not always easy. It is fine for teachers to express ongoing difficulty in dealing with a traumatic event as long as they also convey a sense that recovery is progressing. Students need to have confidence in their teacher's recovery as well as their own. Even the most resilient teachers can become "burned out" by witnessing repeated traumatic incidents.

Teachers can also experience what is known as "vicarious trauma." This happens when teachers experience the depression or anxiety of their students as their own. The signs of trauma are initially invisible because they are caused by what the child experiences in the home, in their neighborhoods, in the halls or in the mind of the students. This trauma gradually builds and increasingly has a negative effect on the classroom environment. This can take a toll on the teacher as these emotions continue to build, especially after a disaster, such as an earthquake or fire.

Traumatic stress caused by school shootings

Three school employees in a northeast Ohio city, two teachers and one administrator, were first hand witnesses to a school shooting. A gunman entered the building and continued to terrorize the school even after the police arrived. The administrator was shot in the leg during the incident. All three continued to work up to two more years after the incident but retired earlier than they had originally planned. Experiencing the shooting caused them to doubt their professional, emotional and physical reasons for continuing to work. None of them felt they could continue as effectively as they had done in the past.

One of the hardest lessons to learn as a teacher is to not take a student's or parent's behavior personally. New teachers must learn how to cope with student emotions as they start their careers. Veteran teachers must learn how to decrease the negative cumulative effects of student tragedies, problems or community disasters and crises. These stressors can have impacts on their mental health over the years. Both new and veteran teachers must work to prevent teacher burnout for themselves and others.

5.4.1 Steps to prevent burnout

Take measures to protect physical security

Being safe allows teachers to feel confident and in control of their environment.

- Be well versed on all the safety procedures in the school
- Know the response procedures to follow during any crisis
- Be alert and pay attention at all times to what is going on in the classroom, the halls, the parking lots, etc.

Engage with colleagues at school

- Become acquainted with the administrators and counselors that also help to take care of the students. Keep them informed of important situations that may lead to violence.
- Find a mentor in the school. Veteran teachers can be an enormous comfort during an anxious time.
- **Do not** hesitate to ask security officers and school resource officers for help

Beware of negative colleagues

- Stay away from complaining, unhappy people

Understand that personal issues will impact school life

◆ Accept the validity of any feelings and stress reactions and work through them at home and at school

Physical problems can affect the quality of a teacher's work

◆ Weight gain, high blood pressure, high cholesterol, alcohol abuse, menopause and other health issues can make it difficult to teach for a full day
   ● Keep abreast of these changes through regular health check-ups
◆ Try to exercise regularly
◆ Eat fresh foods: vegetables, fruit, whole grains, lean protein

Find a way to completely relax

◆ Take vacations
◆ Visit friends, relatives, or take inexpensive bus trips
◆ Read entertaining books that are completely unrelated to teaching
◆ Go to the movies
◆ Exercise

Set new goals or achievements for oneself and the school

◆ Ask administrators for a project that needs doing. Looking for more work is not always popular, but it can help teachers regain momentum.

◆ Help another teacher with a project he/she is working on

Make life enrichment plans
◆ Look around within your district for a different type of job that is related to education
◆ Take a course that is interesting – not one that is required
◆ Go to teachers' workshops and take summer classes that are not just required but are enjoyable
◆ Look for grant opportunities for workshops and professional development
◆ Join teacher associations

Take pride in accomplishments
◆ Realize the good and essential work you do
◆ Praise others for the good job they are doing as well. The kindness will be returned.

5.5 Recovery resources

There are a wide variety of resources available to teachers to help students, and themselves, recover after traumatic incidents. Teachers should not place themselves in the role of a counselor or therapist. But it is important that teachers know where to direct requests for further assistance. Teachers often need recovery assistance themselves. The best place to start is with the mental health professionals at the school or school district who can offer a variety of resources. The school district and teachers union should have programs to assist teachers specifically in the recovery process. Local mental health organizations and hospitals may also be able to give assistance and information to teachers, parents and students. State and Federal government agencies can also provide information resources on recovery. National non-profit and corporate organizations are yet another source.

The following is a short list of organizations that can provide information on the recovery process or offer counseling services.

Federal government

The Federal Emergency Management Agency (FEMA) has published a guide for teachers on how to help students recover entitled, *How to Help Children After a Disaster: A Guidebook for Teachers.*
http://www.fema.gov/kids/tch_help.htm

The National Center for Post-Traumatic Stress Disorder (NCPTSD) of the U.S. Department of Veterans Affairs offers extensive resources on PTSD and how to help children after a disaster.
http://www.ncptsd.org

The Substance Abuse and Mental Health Services Administration (SAMHSA) of the U.S. Department of Health and Human Services offers a number of resources on recovery including guides for parents and teachers for dealing with children after disasters, tips for talking about

traumatic events and other links and references to resources.
http://www.mentalhealth.org/cmhs/TraumaticEvents

Non-profit organizations

The American Psychological Association (APA) in cooperation with the American Red Cross has developed a Disaster Response Network of psychologists trained in disaster response who volunteer their assistance to relief workers, victims, and victims' families after man-made or natural disasters.
http://www.apa.org/practice/drnindex.html

The American Red Cross, through its *Masters of Disaster* program, has published a guide entitled *Facing Fear: Helping Young People Deal With Terrorism and Other Tragic Events*.
http://www.redcross.org/disaster/masters/facingfear/

Suicide Awareness/Voices of Education (SAVE) offers resources for helping adults and children cope with loss and understanding death and suicide.
http://www.save.org/

The National Mental Health Association has developed a series of *Coping with Disaster* fact sheets dealing with general disasters and more specific incidents such as recent hurricanes and military deployments.
http://www.nmha.org/reassurance/anniversary/index.cfm

For-profit organizations

Disaster Training International provides resources and training to assist adults help children recover from disasters.
http://www.disastertraining.org/

Prepare, Respond, Recover offers consulting services, conferences and online training manuals to instruct others how to help with recovery efforts.
http://www.prepareresponderecover.com/index.html

See *6.6 Recovery curriculum development* for ideas on creating units for students to learn about the causes and lessons learned from large-scale emergencies.

NOTES

Chapter 6

How can teachers encourage students to help with school safety?

6.1 Introduction

Teachers are responsible for helping students understand that everyone in a school should be alert and work together to maintain a safe learning environment. Teachers should strive for a proper balance between informing and alarming. It is also important to keep in mind that students are variably sensitive to safety information: one student may be unaffected while another may become panicked. Students that trust teachers are more likely to help avert dangerous situations.

In this regard, teachers are advised to try to follow the general guidelines:

- Learn about students' personal, family and community experiences
- With the assistance and approval from school administrators, create and administer a confidential questionnaire to measure student life style and background
- Use classroom activities to encourage dialogue about school safety
- Assign students to write journal entries about potential or past incidents at school
- Practice student responses to different kinds of emergencies. Activities such as quietly lining up at the door are quick and can be performed at any time during the school day.

Chapter overview

This chapter will describe ways that teachers can build trust and raise safety awareness with students in a responsible manner, and will discuss in-depth the following aspects:

◆   Building trust
◆   Raising safety awareness
◆   Teaching school safety lessons
◆   Using classroom aids
◆   Sample recovery lesson plans

6.2 Building trust

It is important for teachers to establish a level of trust with students so that they feel comfortable confiding their problems. Viewing each student as an individual with a life outside the walls of the classroom is essential. Students regularly seek advice from teachers and school administrators on how to live their lives and solve problems. Motivated by fear and seeking help, many students will talk with teachers about personal problems. Teachers should be conscious not to step into the role of a school counselor or psychologist. Instead, teachers should serve as the student's link with the school to help to prevent or stop an ongoing problem that could lead to a violent incident.

Teachers should think about the following concerns when trying to build the trust of students:

Building trust with students helps them feel comfortable confiding problems **2004**/0564630

- ◆ **Respect students' request for confidentiality**. Many times the information – not the source – is the most important tool for the school administration. If the student's life is in danger, however, it may be necessary to disregard confidentiality.
- ◆ **Reveal examples of personal problems**. Sometimes sharing a few personal problems and asking for suggestions for the solution shows the students respect for their judgment. For example, sharing classroom decisions connected with choice of materials, projects, scheduling of deadlines gives students ownership and shows respect for their ideas.
- ◆ **Share past incidents involving unnamed former students.** This shows compassion as a teacher and sets

the stage for students to take their own initiative and
approach the teacher with problems.

♦   **Show compassion when students request more time
    to complete a project or are absent from school**. Even
    if the student does not share the reason for the request at
    that time, allow for a reasonable extension. Students
    may have problems at home beyond their control.

♦   **Show respect to earn respect and build trust.** Adults
    sometimes forget that showing respect to youths can be a
    powerful means to gain trust and build confidence.
    Teachers who recall past adult role models will probably
    remember that these people were easier to trust and
    communicate with.

Frustrated students frequently engage in fights or altercations
in the school and/or the neighborhood. These suggestions for
building trust can alleviate frustration and hopelessness that
could lead to violence in the classroom. In addition, students
who are confident in a teacher's ability to respond are more
likely to follow directions or provide information/assistance
in the event of an emergency.

6.2.1 Listening and talking to students

Students bring emotional baggage into the classroom no
matter how hard they try to avoid it. Listening to students is
fundamental in understanding student perspectives and
challenges that affect their personal lives at home and at
school. By listening and talking to students, teachers can
come to understand and begin to lessen their fears, anxieties

and vulnerabilities that can lead to a school emergency, such as a violent incident. Understanding these student traits could also help teachers defuse violence related to community spillover and domestic abuse that might occur.

Making students understand and accept the risks to the classroom from the hazards the school is likely to face may give them a sense of control and may help lessen anxiety about these events. This can help to create a more effective learning environment. In addition, discussing and learning about potential emergency response measures will definitely make a response to one of these incidents more efficient. Dedicated teachers who were willing to listen have averted student violence towards others at school, such as school shootings, and violence to themselves, such as with suicide.

Of course, this means actively listening to students and, when appropriate, asking questions to prompt students to talk about issues that may be difficult for them to share. Research shows that a significant number of chronically bullied students never tell a single adult about the bullying while they are in school. As in other aspects of their jobs, by actively listening, teachers truly have the power to affect students' lives in significant ways.

6.2.2 Personal, family and community issues
At any time, a teacher may hear a story from a student about his/her personal, family and/or community life. These may include stories about his/her own criminal activity,

relationship problems, family problems, neighborhood conflicts, gang activity, extended family discord and/or job problems. Teachers should listen without passing judgment. If it seems that a situation has the potential to become violent, teachers may need to share this information with a counselor, an administrator or a school resource officer. Students who are having health problems or legal problems may not know where to go for help. This frustration may build to a point where the student lashes out at innocent victims or him/herself.

Sometimes, the student's home life can make life difficult for the student; parental divorce, alcoholism, drugs and neglect can drastically affect the ability of students to learn. Teachers should remember that each student has unique problems. Not listening and responding can make students feel like they are alone in the world. These feelings, left unnoticed, can manifest themselves in violence directed against themselves or other students.

In addition, the overall climate of the community can also feed into feelings of helplessness. Many problems from the community spill over into the classroom. Teachers should understand the community from which the student population is drawn to better help affected students deal with these problems and focus on learning.

Teachers should also learn about positive organizations within the community. There are many agencies, clubs, and centers that serve as positive resources for the members of the community. For example, Boys and Girls Clubs have a demonstrated positive impact on inner city youth. The Boys Scouts, Girl Scouts and the YWCA have safe places for students to spend time after school. School districts that have evening neighborhood centers in their schools perform a great service by providing open gyms, pools, classes and safe places for students to spend their time. Many ethnic neighborhoods have cultural clubs that provide healthy environments and reinforce cultural connections. Teachers need to become familiar with these places to suggest them to students and if possible attend functions where their students participate.

6.3 Raising safety awareness

Teachers must create an awareness of the importance of classroom safety with their students. Adding the eyes and ears of students in the classroom can multiply the effective-ness of established safety procedures. If students can assist teachers by spotting unsafe school conditions, suggesting improved response procedures or noticing violent tendencies in fellow students, classroom and school safety will be en-hanced immeasurably. Student drills on emergency response procedures will help maintain calm in the event of an emer-gency and even save lives. To accomplish this goal, teachers should incorporate safety into everyday classroom lessons.

There are a variety of ways that teachers can raise the level of safety awareness in the classroom, including the following activities:

- Hold safety campaigns in the classroom
- Invite public safety and emergency response officials to the classroom to speak on safety related topics
- Create a sample emergency scenario and discuss how students would and should react to the event
- Perform regular drills for a variety of potential hazards to the class

6.4 School safety lessons

Teachers can use school lessons to teach general safety concepts to students and accustom them to discussions about possible emergency plans. If a school has recently faced a particular emergency, a school lesson can be a positive way to return the classroom to a safe learning environment. Teachers can use the following suggested activities to incorporate safety discussions in their lesson plans.

6.4.1 Questionnaires

Some teachers have found that a good starting point to assess what students know about school safety is to have them fill out a questionnaire. School officials and teachers may want to do this activity at the beginning of the school year or as a part of new student orientation. Studies have shown that these activities can be very revealing. Teachers are advised to include a variety of questions, such as favorite books, movies, televisions shows as well as ones dealing explicitly with school safety. This combination can set students at ease. After the students complete their answers, have a round table discussion to allow the students to voice how they feel about school safety. This can also be a prompt for a writing assignment that will allow reticent students to also reveal their feelings and thoughts. Teachers should be sure to follow any guidelines the school system has in place for the use of surveys and questionnaires.

6.4.2 Sample activities

This section presents sample activities teachers can use to involve students in maintaining a safe classroom. Activities teaching school safety can be used to teach standard learning concepts, such as research and writing.

NOTE: Before using these examples, teachers should ensure that planned activities are in accordance with school policies.

Activity 1
Journal writing

Teachers can direct students to write about their personal feelings during evacuation after a particular emergency – fire, student violence, bomb threat, and human-caused disasters/ accidents. Ask students what the school district could have done differently to make the entire experience less traumatic.

Discussion

Share and discuss these journals during class anonymously.

Journal activities can help draw out students' feelings and concerns about school safety   **2004**/0564606

Activity 2

Teachers can brainstorm with students about what they would put into an emergency response kit.

- ◆ Hold a scavenger hunt with items in the classroom that should be included in the kit. Talk about why each item is important.
- ◆ Ask if each classroom should have the same items
- ◆ Ask the students if they would feel safer if each room had an emergency response kit

Activity 3

Teachers can simulate different situations with students about reporting worrying behavior in other students. For example, ask when it is better to speak out when a student may become violent than when to keep silent. Teachers should divide students into small groups to write specific scenarios with one ending in tragedy and the other ending in conflict resolution.

Activity 4

Teachers may want to invite police officers, fire fighters, emergency medical personnel and other emergency responders into the classroom. Before they arrive, students can write questions about their careers and duties. Having the questions written ahead of time provides a sense of order for the classroom environment and gives the guests time to prepare answers.

Activity 5

Teachers can allow students time to discuss certain emergency situations that have occurred in their lives. If a classmate has been hurt or killed, this may be a time of healing and mourning. Often young people will feel more comfortable sharing their feelings with friends and teachers than with their own families.

Activity 6

Teachers can instruct students to compile a school safety portfolio based on classroom activities. This could include a section for suggestions for school administrators as the results of a survey conducted by students in their school and community. Artwork, photographs, newspaper and magazine articles could be included as the year progresses.

6.4.3 Sample school safety awareness lesson plan

The following is a sample school safety lesson plan teachers can use to promote a safe classroom while teaching writing and reading skills. As most state educational standards can be met through a variety of approaches, this particular lesson plan can be embedded in the curriculum and should be tailored to meet the required writing instruction guidelines of the school district. Teachers can modify this lesson plan for use with different age groups, paying attention to the standards required for each grade level.

Directions

Students will write a well-organized composition about how school safety affects their lives.

Format

Instruct students to write a five-paragraph composition with an introduction, three body paragraphs expanding on specific ideas and a concluding paragraph based on their ideas about school safety. Using their journals, experiences from their lives or a news article, students should write coherent, well-organized paragraphs.

Introduction - Paragraph I

Begin with a hook or catchy lead to attract the readers' attention. This can be an anecdote, recent event or a statistic about school safety.

State the main idea in a thesis statement that includes three details that will be developed in the composition:

Three supporting details

A:

B:

C:

Paragraph II

Discuss detail A

Paragraph III

Discuss detail B

Paragraph IV

Discuss detail C

Paragraph V

Conclusion: Restate the thesis statement in different words. End with a quote, lesson to be learned or another anecdote that summarizes the three details from the composition.

Figure 6.1 Sample graphic organizer for sample school safety lesson plan

Lesson procedure

The teacher will introduce the topic of school safety awareness. Students will brainstorm ideas about their school or write in their journals. A news article dealing with a recent school safety event could be introduced and discussed at this time.

Handout

Students can use the graphic organizer in Figure 6.1 as a handout to decide on information they want to write.

6.5 Classroom aids

Training and education about school safety is recommended for teachers and students throughout the school year. One way to accomplish this is to have classroom aids and emergency checklists properly displayed in the classroom. These aids will serve as a constant reminder to students and staff of what to do in the event of a crisis. Advanced planning can ensure that an emergency response is more effective during the actual event. All teachers and students can do their part to contribute to school safety.

6.5.1 Putting together an emergency response kit

Most school districts have a variety of emergency kits that assist in the response to an incident. If resources allow, teachers should keep their own emergency response kits that are specific to the needs of their classrooms. They are meant to be useful in any type of emergency and for the teacher to take during an evacuation. Teachers should keep their response kit in a readily accessible, but secure, location. The following are recommended items for a classroom emergency response kit:

- Flashlight
- Sterile gloves
- Water
- Tissue paper
- Emergency rain ponchos
- Lockdown plan and procedures
- Diagram of the school
- Roster of your students
- Emergency contact/medical information for students (as consistent with school privacy policies)
- Student release forms (as consistent with school privacy policies)
- First aid kit
- Cell phone (if provided by school) or coins for a payphone
- Emergency radio (if provided by school)
- A copy of the ready reference flip chart

6.5.2 Ready reference flip chart

A ready reference flip chart that details emergency response procedures can serve as a guide for classroom activities as well as emergency response. Each section of the flip chart could be used for the following activities:

- A prompt for classroom discussion
- A prompt for an expository essay
- An Internet research project
- A project doing research in magazines for pictures of equipment that could be used to help with an emergency response
- An activity for small groups to recommend additional or modify existing response procedures for one or several emergencies
- An activity for small groups to teach a response procedure to the entire class

6.5.3 Posters

Information from posters has been known to save people's lives. Ordinary citizens, such as teachers and students, have observed posters detailing CPR procedures or the Heimlich maneuver allowing them to prevent tragedies. Each school district has different standards and regulations regarding the display of posters and each may issue a standardized safety poster. The school administration should inform teachers about specific criteria related to displaying safety posters.

It may be a learning experience for a class to research and produce safety awareness posters. Students can learn a significant amount of practical safety information by conducting their own research and creating their own posters. Possible poster topics can include any of the topics in the ready reference flip chart.

Student keeps teacher alive with CPR

A student from an inner city high school was riding the city bus to school one day when her gym teacher who was also on the bus, had a heart attack. Because she knew CPR that she had learned at school, she was able to keep him alive until the EMS arrived.

Teachers must ensure that each poster created is consistent with the school's approved emergency response procedures in order to avoid any mistakes during an actual crisis situation. In turn, teachers should review student drafts of the information to be used before they create the actual poster.

Teachers can use the following techniques when assigning students the task of making classroom safety posters:

♦   Have students do research in the school library and on the Internet about safety measures
♦   Invite local law enforcement officers and emergency responders to make a presentation on safety. Have the students create posters as a follow-up.
♦   Collaborate with an art teacher to create a unit on school safety through the visual arts
♦   Offer a school-wide contest to choose the best school safety posters. Display posters in a central location and allow students to vote on the best ones.

6.5.4 Classroom safety checklists

As with creating posters, creating safety checklists can be an excellent activity to help students learn safety procedures in a creative fashion. Teachers can assign the following activities regarding classroom safety checklists:

◆ An Internet research project by students looking at sample checklists used by schools around the nation. State departments of education may be a good starting place.

◆ Group presentations based on interviews with members of the school staff and emergency responders concluding with a recommended classroom safety checklist

◆ A classroom presentation by law enforcement and public safety personnel

◆ Research by students on safety considerations for different parts of the country (i.e. earthquake, hurricane, or tornado-prone areas) and specialized checklists for these areas

Again, it is important that checklists presented by students be consistent with the school's emergency operations and response plans. Please see the inside front cover of this guide for sample checklists.

6.6 Recovery curriculum development

After large scale incidents, such as a civil disturbance, terrorist attack or a natural disaster, teachers may consider creating a lesson on teaching the causes and lessons learned from these incidents. The following are examples from recent events where teachers have created lessons by combining print and other media to enhance textbooks, readings, special projects and other assignments.

6.6.1 Los Angeles riots

After the civil unrest of 1992 in South Central Los Angeles, the Constitutional Rights Foundation commissioned a curriculum written by attorney Marshall Croddy. The lessons were based on civil rights legislation and the federal case against the LAPD officers who were accused of violating Rodney King's civil rights during the videotaped beatings in Los Angeles.

6.6.2 Oklahoma City bombing

Mr. Croddy and the Constitutional Rights Foundation also produced a series of lessons on terrorism in the United States in the aftermath of the bombing of the Murrah Federal Building in Oklahoma City. Utilizing a chronology of federal laws enacted in response to terrorist acts in the United States, the lessons were organized around law-related readings, followed by classroom discussions. They included a detailed guide for teachers and opportunities for lawyers to speak in history and social studies classrooms.

6.6.3 Northridge earthquake

In 1994, the Los Angeles Unified School District used curricula developed by the Federal Emergency Management

The 1994 Northridge earthquake impacted students and teachers in the Los Angeles Unified School District
2003/0564502

Agency (FEMA), entitled "Disaster Dudes," to help students recover from the devastating earthquakes in their area. The lessons focused on helping students understand the widespread effects of natural disasters and how to best recover from events such as the Northridge Earthquake.

6.6.4 World Trade Center/Pentagon terrorist attacks

The United Federation of Teachers in New York City organized a resource guide for teachers after the terrorist attack and collapse of the World Trade Center Towers on September 11, 2001. A special feature was material that could be used to educate students on issues of diversity, ways to combat hate crimes and discrimination and lessons in values education.

Source: *Jane's School Safety Handbook, Second Edition*

NOTES

NOTES

<u>NOTES</u>

NOTES